The Measure of a Gene

A Modest Proposal on the Meaning of Life

David Allan Smith

VANTAGE PRESS
New York

For my mother and father,
Emma Liberty Wildman Smith
and Charles Henry Smith

Ideas are cheap, David.

Herschel Roman, 1969

CONTENTS

ACKNOWLEDGMENT

The quotation from the writings of H. J. Muller, appearing on page 43, is reprinted with permission from *The American Naturalist*, published by the University of Chicago Press, copyright:

New York
The Science Press
1922

Prolog

Astonishment is a high energy state. Perhaps we often behave in a glib and facile manner, instead of an astonished manner, as a respite from fatigue. We take for granted, then, things like atoms of hydrogen when we should be surprised anew each day that we know hydrogen is there. It is even more remarkable that we know hydrogen has a nucleus—a single proton—and a single electron somewhere in orbit around that nucleus. We toss off this astonishing bit of intelligence as if it were trivia, and yet surely we alone on this earth, and conceivably in the universe, know of it. Worse, we have little chance of exhorting ourselves to truly understand things we treat as trivia. Too rarely do we get to feel the special peace that accompanies a moment of understanding or insight. At such moments, life seems less like the imposition it is, and more like the gift that it also is.

On the other hand, the same faculties that can present us with the joy of understanding just as easily confront us with the agony of doubt. This is nowhere more apparent than on the question of our origin. The human capacity to realize the logical necessity of origin—we do not at present suspect that any other animal does this—simultaneously raises the specter of meaning attached to that origin. Humans generally do not like to contemplate, and may even be threatened by, the proposition that life has no meaning. Any model that proposes life to be an accident in the cosmos tends to have passionate adversaries and few adherents.

While the subject of life's meaning is and will surely remain controversial for some time to come, there remains no meaningful debate about the major outlines of life's mechanisms. Biological information is stored and transmitted in macromolecules, the nucleic acids, RNA and DNA. Information is expressed primarily in the form of macromolecules known as proteins. These, in turn, marshal other categories of molecules, including carbohydrates and lipids, to the service of biological systems. There is much yet to be learned about mechanisms at levels of higher complexity (consider the immune system, embryological development and neurobiology as examples) but the rate of increase in our understanding is so rapid that even specialists struggle to stay abreast of the information in their own fields.

There also remains no meaningful debate about the origin of life on this planet. It is very old—on the order of four billion years—and has continuity from those distant beginnings to all of today's surviving forms, including the most complex. There are lively debates about the identities of players in the transition from proto-life to life, about the historical roles of RNA and DNA, and about constancy of evolutionary rates. But these debates are about mode and tempo of Darwinian evolution, not the fact of Darwinian evolution.

2

In spite of the profound knowledge that now exists for the first two branches in the biological triad–those of mechanism and origin—biologists remain timid on the subject of the third branch, that of meaning. The most knowledgeable biologists rarely utter a word about the meaning of life, ceding interpretation in this area to mysticism and mythology. Mechanism and origin are studied by one methodology—the scientific method—while meaning is contemplated by a different approach altogether. The resulting schism is ready for change.

The rationale for a biology-based examination of the meaning of life is quite straightforward. On the presumption that there is meaning attached to life, and life is not just an accident in the cosmos, the expression of that meaning occurs through biological mechanisms. It is peculiar in the extreme to talk about what something means without first coming to terms with what that something is. Whatever life may mean, that meaning is expressed through life's mechanisms. Meanwhile, the existing body of thought, teaching and even dogma on the subject of meaning is archaic, having been devised in virtually complete ignorance of biological mechanisms and origins. It is inevitable that the issue be joined. Ultimately, we will be driven to explore it systematically.

This monograph addresses the question of meaning by asking if there is a single, unifying theme running through the origin and evolution of life. If there is a unitary theme—and we can trace it seamlessly through the history of life—it then becomes sensible to ask if the theme itself is the meaning (or the key to meaning). There does indeed exist such a theme, and it does indeed suggest its own meaning, as we shall presently see.

One of the most productive approaches to the study of biology has been to focus on the structure and function of genes. Since genes are the vehicles of information transfer from one generation to the next, the study of genes provides a sort of ringside seat to what biological information is, and how it gets expressed. We will consider biological mechanisms and origins largely from the genetic point of view, and then use this point of view as our perspective on meaning.

If this approach seems interesting, please read on. However, to anyone not accustomed to thinking about life in terms of the transmission and expression of genes, some of the text will be moderately challenging. It may coincidentally prove rewarding to those who would like to know more on the subject. All facets of gene function are treated at a level of technical detail intended to be informative but readable. The text is supplemented by a set of appendixes which some readers might find useful.

As occurs with any specialty, genetics is well adorned with misconceptions. One of these is the

4

recently popular but peculiar and unworkable idea that genes are selfish. The idea of gene selfishness does not simply fail to describe the properties of genes—the idea is exactly wrong. In some of its applications it is absurdly wrong. We will show instead that genes represent eons of discovery. Their history is that of successive approximations to the truth. Confusing the history of discovery with an act of selfishness demeans the real legacy of genes. A successful gene tells a truth.

Some of what follows is speculative. This is not difficult to recognize where it occurs. When ideas and opinions of others are employed, this will be indicated by a parenthetical listing of the author's name and the date of the publication (e.g., Gould, 1989). This source will be found in the bibliography (e.g., *Wonderful Life*). The bibliography is small and eclectic by design, containing general sources such as textbooks, monographs such as the Gould book mentioned above, and a few citations of the original literature where the subject matter is either current and heating up (origin of life studies fall into this category) or classical and deserving of another look. Quotations are used sparingly—because of budget constraints, it has simply been necessary to avoid dealing with copyright issues.

Ideas and opinions that are not accompanied by a citation are either in the public domain or presumably mine, but I am not always sure the ideas I think are mine are, in fact, original. However, any nonsense is absolutely mine, since I have the option of recognizing and correcting or omitting it.

1. Towards a Unified Theory of Life

A scant three or four centuries ago, the Western imagination was dominated by a static universe with the earth at its center. Humans were thought to have been specially created to occupy the central position on this central stage.

We now know ourselves to be in an expanding universe of indescribable proportions. Earth is an infinitesimally small part of this universe. It has even been demoted from the central position in its own small solar system. Indeed, it is a modest satellite flying at unremarkable velocity around a mediocre star.

The proud occupants of this satellite have received other news, equally startling and even closer to home. Their mighty continents are drifting about the globe, and they themselves are descended from something that crawled out of the sea a few thousand millennia ago. Their nearest relatives are chimpanzees. This is a lot of humble pie in a relatively short time.

People often balk at, or recoil from such revelations but go on being curious, asking questions and finding answers. Moreover, humanity continues to find ways to incorporate new facts into the social fabric, even when this results in the displacement of old facts and cherished beliefs. It is fair to ask why we do this to ourselves and why we are so good at adapting to the consequences.

The essay that follows examines this simple proposition: The seemingly inexorable human pursuit of truth is a biological legacy. This legacy is inescapable because life itself is rooted in an inexorable pursuit of truth. Each evolutionary increase in biological complexity represents the discovery of neither more nor less than a new layer of truth. We seek truth as a biological necessity. We embrace truth because it is the foundation of all biological legacy. We are utterly helpless to do otherwise.

Of course, truth can be controversial and tentative. In the human experience, as unlikely as it may now seem, it was apparently once regarded as truth that the earth was flat. In the realm of evolutionary ideas, it was once regarded as truth that *Tyrannosaurus rex* was indomitable. We will examine the proposition that the demise of these guesses about the truth has a common denominator—each was disproven.

The model of life as a pursuit of truth will be constructed in a way that is chronological and cumulative. The logic of the argument will follow the logic of life. We must first visit the idea of patience and grasp the idea of time; it is not possible to get a feeling for the structure of life without first having a feeling for the vastness of time through which life has emerged. We will then trace life through four distinct phases of its development—the sequential mastery of chemistry (chancing upon truth at the atomic and molecular level as a necessity for life), of chemical contingency (the power to vary chemical expression), of physics (chancing upon and incorporating truth at a distance) and of abstraction (chancing upon the contingency of truth at a distance). These levels of mastery parallel (1) the emergence of cells, now arguably perfect vehicles of internalized life, (2) the capacity of one cell to be different things in different settings, (3) the emergence of multicellular structures that externalized life in the sense that the cells in these structures do not have to touch something to know it is there and (4) the emergence of nervous systems that receive information from a distance and transform it at will. Each of these steps is the addition of a new layer of truth upon a pre-existing foundation and, together, they create the basis of our consciousness.

We will end this essay on the arguably provocative note that behind life's four-billion-year pursuit of truth there may very well lie a question—that life began as a question and not as an answer. If we can discern such a question and even begin to answer it, we will probably have discovered what we are and what our lives mean.

2. Cosmological and Darwinian Time

The Life That We Know Is a Four-Billion-Year-Old Experiment on a Five-Billion-Year-Old Planet in a Fifteen-Billion-Year-Old Universe

By definition, a random process can produce anything.
–Jacques Monod, paraphrased.

All episodes of evolutionary change occur in two steps. The first of these is the production of genetic variation. We will later describe the occurrence and nature of such variation, but for now will only note that variation is generated by mutation and that mutation is essentially a chance or random process. In at least this limited respect, it follows that evolution is a chance or random process. None of this implies meaninglessness.

The second component of Darwinian evolution, Natural Selection, simply scrutinizes this chance variation. Variation that is deleterious to the system in which it occurs is eliminated. Variants that are beneficial and, in some cases, variants that open doors to new opportunities are woven into the fabric of life. Once established, these variants change the system in which they've been included and, thus, become necessary to that system.

Developing an intellectual grasp of this duality—contemporaneous genetic necessities having arisen as past chance events—is one of the central challenges to understanding the origin and nature of life. The challenge is all the more formidable given

10

the large array and complexity of living systems. Clearly, for chance events to be the ultimate source of all the life forms we now see, such chance events must have been occurring across vast amounts of time. It is in this context that we turn to the cosmologists, the paleontologists and the geologists. They have, in fact, revolutionized our view of life by demonstrating exactly the expanse of time required to make sense of necessity arising from chance. They have given us a litany about time that stands at the core of our understanding: we now see life to be a four-billion-year-long experiment on a five-billion-year-old planet in an eight-to-fifteen-billion-year-old universe—the cosmologists are still working on the latter measurement. Since time, in billions of years, is conceptually difficult for most of us, this litany becomes a sort of mantra. Without it, one can know life but never understand it.

We humans encounter another conceptual difficulty when thinking about the origin of life, this one concerning the nature of evidence and the process of thinking about evidence. Since we extol the virtues of evidence, let us examine ourselves and, in particular, the constancy of our thought processes in the gathering and assessment of evidence.

Consider an atom of hydrogen, to our knowledge the simplest element in the universe. The nucleus of the most common form or isotope of hydrogen consists of a single proton. A single electron orbits around this nucleus. Hydrogen gas, one of the common constituents of earth's atmosphere, is a molecule consisting of two hydrogen atoms covalently bonded to each other. As an example of a slightly more complex molecule, consider water—it contains two hydrogen atoms bonded to an atom of oxygen (H–O–H). A chemist will tell you that the angle formed by the two bonds is 105 degrees rather than 180 degrees (that is, the molecule is not linear) and explains this angle in terms of unpaired electrons.

No one has ever seen an atom of hydrogen or a molecule of water, the bonds that exist in such a molecule or the electrons involved in those bonds. Yet we accept the reality of these constructs. They were discovered through application of the methodology we all refer to as science. That methodology instructed us that electrons, atoms, molecules and bonds exist as we say they do.

Our models of elements such as hydrogen and oxygen, and compounds like water, have led to predictions about how they should behave in various settings. Those predictions have been abundantly tested—again through the methodology we call science—and repeatedly validated. Hydrogen, oxygen and the rest of the elements of the periodic table are real. Electrons are real. Chemical bonds are real. Our ability to know the existence of and properties of these invisible things is testimony to the power of the methodology.

The powerful methodology of science has also informed us about biological evolution. Many people accept these findings in the same spirit as they accept the existence, size and mass of a hydrogen atom. Oddly, however, many people do not, accepting the rules of evidence when they tell us about hydrogen, but rejecting those same rules of evidence when they tell us about evolution. In place of rules of evidence, they invoke ancient sources. This amounts to learning chemistry and physics from modern texts, and biology from texts cobbled together in ignorance.

Unfortunately, while this set of circumstances may be quaint, it cannot lead us to an understanding of who and what we are. Understanding, we know with certainty, comes from inquiry and the rigorous application of rules of evidence. Denial of evolution, accomplished by suspending rules of evidence, is thus an intellectual sleight-of-hand that collapses under the weight of its own illogic. If we hope to understand ourselves, we are constrained to treat evolution with the same rigor and standards we apply to every other discipline. If we fail to understand ourselves through rigorous inquiry, we reduce ourselves to a cartoon.

On October 2nd, 1836, Charles Darwin returned to England on *H.M.S. Beagle* after nearly five years abroad as ship's naturalist. He carried ashore the seeds of one of the great revolutions in science. He was not quick, however, to announce his theory of Natural Selection as the motive force of evolution. He had other things on his mind. Rather than being occupied with life on earth, Darwin was consumed with thoughts about the earth itself.

Darwin's long voyage was an intersection of events destined to reshape our lives. He had taken aboard, and proceeded to read, the most modern geology text of the day (Lyell's *Principles of Geology*), but supplemented his reading with his own observations, especially on numerous trips ashore in South America. Equipped with these two sources of information, Darwin began a systematic reappraisal of the then prevailing view that the earth was static. The depth of his absorption with the changeability of earth's surface is clearly seen in the choice of topic for his first scholarly publication to result from that trip. Employing the geological phenomena of uplift and subsidence, he invented and published a model for the formation of coral reefs. It remains the standard model to this day. Darwin had begun to see clearly that the earth is subject to dramatic change and that it had been undergoing such change for a very long time. We take such things as mountain building for granted today. In Darwin's day, geological phenomena were coming into focus for a very small school of thought and he was at the cutting edge of that school.

There was, of course, an important distinction between Darwin and the other contemporary students of geology. Only Darwin was also collecting and cataloging the plants and animals he observed in the

14

various places he visited. As he collected and observed biological specimens, noting that specimens from different regions differed from each other, while simultaneously noting the instability of the earth, he began thinking about the regional differences between his specimens in the context of changes in the earth itself. This conjunction of changing earth with changing life was to become a major factor in the strength of the Darwinian method and a central reason that his work has withstood the test of time so remarkably intact.

The first explicit record of Darwin's synthesis of thoughts about an evolving earth as home to evolving life began in July of 1837. Nine months after his return on the *Beagle* and his immersion in thoughts about terrestrial instability, Darwin began the first of his notebooks on "the transmutation of species." His most famous work, *On the Origin of Species*, would not appear for another twenty years. In those twenty years, Darwin first sought to reconcile a changing earth, and especially earth's changed places, with the distribution of life forms. In other words, he was inventing the analysis of the cause and effect relationships between new habitat creation and the evolution of organisms that came to occupy those places.

The classical example of this new field, Darwinian biogeography, is his report on the Galápagos Islands. He observed that these islands were younger than the closest mainland, that the organisms on the islands were unique to the islands but similar to those on the mainland and consisted only of those that could swim, float or fly there. In short, changes in the earth (island building) had created a new niche which could be colonized by those who could travel to it. Secondly, the modern inhabitants of the new niche were related to, but evolutionarily different from, the original colonizers. This process of change is iterative in a manner first discerned by Darwin and operates on these properties of organisms and their habitats:

1. Organisms exist in populations.
2. Any given population of organisms occupies a more or less defined niche within its range.
3. All populations contain variation; not all individuals in a population are identical. Thus, a species has a general type, not an archetype.
4. All populations produce more offspring than will survive. Survivors tend to be those most well adapted to the niche. Differential survival is mediated by Natural Selection.
5. Niches change.
6. This process is iterative, generation after generation.

This short paraphrase of Darwin's Laws, while not precise or exhaustive, is accurate and adequate. In a place like the Galápagos Islands, the

16

manifestation of the iteration of Darwinian Law is that, over time, derived populations diverge from their ancestral populations and ultimately consist of derivative organisms. We see this biological pattern wherever we can document this kind of geological change. The implication is clear that there is great value in the capacity of biological systems to change.

One of our main goals will be to show how Darwinian Law is rooted in genetic law; Darwinian evolution is the observed phenomenon, but it is the behavior of genes that provides the mechanism by which evolution occurs. If we seek to understand life, and such understanding requires understanding how life came to be, it also requires understanding the transmission of the genes that define the legacy of life. In other words, understanding the legacy of life requires understanding change, and in all biological systems, including ourselves, it is genes that change.

The study of genes, however, was a late arrival in the history of human thinking about biological evolution. There were in place three well-developed branches of evolutionary thought by the time genes were recognized as important in the process. One of these was biogeography, the study of the distribution of organisms we touched on above; it is one of the linchpins of Darwinian biology.

We tend to think of biogeography in terms of the distribution of organisms across space. As we have seen, however, biogeography is also a function of distribution in time. Cause and effect relationships, such as those between organisms and their habitats, cannot occur in a static system—a causal thing must always occur in advance of an effected thing. That is, we cannot think about Darwinian biogeography while ignoring Darwinian time. Biogeography must be seen in the context of time as well as space.

A second branch of pre-genetic evolutionary thought grew out of the discovery of fossils and the ensuing study of the fossil record. Beginning with the ground-breaking work of Cuvier in the early nineteenth century, it has been known that a succession of life forms has populated the earth. Until Darwin, however, these observations were largely rationalized to fit non-evolutionary explanations. Even Darwin, while recognizing the significance of fossils in an evolutionary context, still worried that the rarity of transitional forms cast doubt on the model of evolution by Natural Selection—the fossil record at first glance appears to be discontinuous. This worry seems a little odd in retrospect, since the remarkable thing about the fossil record is that there are any fossils at all.

Fortunately, since the time of Darwin, the erstwhile gaps in the fossil record have been slowly filling. One of the more dramatic and beautiful transitional forms is a reptile-bird known as *Archaeopteryx* (for accuracy, we should note that Darwin knew of *Archaeopteryx* and included it in *The Origin of Species*). *Archaeopteryx* and other, related fossil forms were essentially small dinosaurs with

18

wings and feathers. They serve as a bridge to an understanding of the observation that skeletons of modern birds appear, on morphological grounds, to be related to skeletons of dinosaurs. It does not follow from this that *Archaeopteryx* itself is an actual ancestor to birds, but only that it was in that branch of dinosauran evolution. There are other candidate ancestors, including one known as *Protoavis*, discovered as recently as 1986. *Protoavis*, at 225 million years old, is some 75 million years older than the known *Archaeopteryx* fossils. Although our understanding of the reptile-to-bird transition is still unfolding, Darwinian biology rests easy—transition-form candidates are in hand.

An equally compelling story of transitional forms occurs in our own lineage with the recent developments in the paleontology of the *Australopithecines* and early species of the genus *Homo*. A good case in point is the very readable description by Leaky and Lewin (1992) of their group's discovery of a *Homo erectus* specimen near Lake Turkana in Kenya. In brief, they unearthed a nearly complete one-and-one-half-million-year-old skeleton of a nine-year-old male (it is worth reading the book just to learn how Leaky and colleagues know the age of this individual at the time of his death). This fellow stood an amazing 5'8" in height, walked bolt-upright and had a brain case about midway in size between modern apes and humans.

Many previously discovered but partial skeletons of *Homo erectus* had suggested their transitional status--fully developed bipedal locomotion like our own associated with intermediate brain size accompanied by modest technological and cultural development. The "Turkana Boy" skeleton is one of a number of recent findings that pull together and solidify our knowledge of the transition from ape-like ancestor to modern humans.

Even though *Archaeopteryx* and *Homo erectus* are astonishing, they cannot eclipse the specimens from the fossil beds known as the Burgess Shale. These 500 million-year-old deposits contain a cornucopia of fossils from the Cambrian explosion— the apparently sudden first appearance of multicellular ancestors to all of today's fauna. The discovery and study of the Burgess fossils have been chronicled by Gould (1989) in a book that should be on every reading list.

An overview goes something like this: Before the Cambrian explosion, the fossil record contains only unicellular organisms and several groups of extremely simple multicellular organisms. The latter, dating from about 700 million years ago, apparently have no modern descendants. Somewhere in the geological window between 700 and 500 million years ago, the ancestral forms of modern animals—from worms to grasshoppers to elephants—made their appearance as if all at once. The oldest known fossilized remains of these animals are in beds generally about 540 million years old. Their appearance in the fossil record really does look as if they exploded onto the scene. The animals of the Burgess Shale were typically one to four inches long (roughly 25 to 100mm) with the exception of a creature called *Anomalocaris,* which was as much as two feet or 600mm in length.

The Burgess Shale does not, however, contain just the story of the ancestry of surviving animal life. It also contains a host of forms (body plans), some described by students of the Burgess as weird or bizarre, that have no modern descendants. In other words, evolution took a mighty leap at the transition from single-cellular to multicellular existence; the products of this leap were subsequently winnowed down to a small number of surviving types.

It should not surprise us in the least, given the history of science, that the Burgess Shale provides answers to some of our questions about evolution while pointing up new questions we hadn't been prepared to ask. In particular, the characteristics of the Burgess fauna, revealing the sudden appearance of a great diversity of life, only to have most of it disappear, suggest to some students of life that evolution does not follow the sort of smooth and consistent path as essentially envisioned by Darwin. Instead, these students argue, evolution is subject to fits and starts. This view, under the modern name of punctuated equilibrium, is thoroughly developed by Gould (1989), who is one of its leading champions.

We will, a little later on, take great pleasure in quibbling with the idea of punctuated equilibrium on the grounds that it is overly dependent on visual criteria.

The controversy surrounding the punctuated equilibrium model of evolution has been interpreted in some quarters to mean that there is evidence contradicting Darwinian evolution. Let us be clear that the argument is about how evolution occurs and not whether evolution occurs.

There is one last type of fossil that has become an essential part of any survey, however brief. These are the stromatolites, layers of sedimentary rock that represent the fossilized remains of microbial organisms that grew in calm and shallow waters. The recognition that these sediments have a fossil origin seems almost like science fiction.

The first step in this recognition was the realization that the structure of stromatolites has a striking resemblance to the structure of a particular modern product of bacterial growth known as a microbial mat. Microbial mats are produced in a number of aquatic environments, including shallow brines, that may be similar to the sites from which the fossil stromatolites originated.

The inspired second step was to realize that the mat-like sedimentary rocks, if they are ancient versions of microbial mats, should contain fossils of the putative microbial organisms that produced them.

Thus, samples of these rocks were cut into thin sections and polished. The thin sections were then placed under a microscope and scanned for fossil imprints of the cells that, according to the hypothesis of microbial origin, should be there. Remarkably, these rocks do contain fossilized cells. Stromatolites are, indeed, fossil versions of microbial mats.

The rationale for seeking, and the technology for seeing, these fossil cells should give all of us pause for admiration. But we are quickly distracted by the spine-tingling result of determining geological ages of stromatolites; they are as much as three and one-half billion years old.[1] Since these fossils represent the remains of cells, and evolution must have had a pre-cellular stage, we infer that the origin of life on this earth occurred on the order of four billion years ago. We are once again confronted with the task of comprehending measures of time beyond any realm of experience. We are simultaneously reminded that a discussion of the fossil record, like a discussion of biogeography, is inseparable from a discussion of time.

Studies of biogeography and the fossil record are two of the classical pillars of the Darwinian view of life. Both of these disciplines measure events across time. A third pillar, comparative studies, may at first seem independent of time. For example, in comparative anatomy, one can assess the similarities of the bones in the forelimbs of existing animals like cats, horses and whales. Similarly, noting the close homologies of embryological structures in, say, developing chickens, mice and pigs could be construed as a strictly contemporary view of relatedness. It is obvious, of course, that one can only make sense of these measures in terms of descent. The comparisons of bones and embryos has us looking for common ancestors and, therefore, has us peering back in time.

More recently, comparative studies have been reinforced by the addition of biochemical and molecular methods. It is now a commonplace to measure the chemical relatedness of homologous molecules from different species (the blood protein hemoglobin from humans, compared to hemoglobin from mice, is an example of homology at the level of proteins). The chemical relatedness is then used to assess phylogenetic relatedness. These methodologies have proven so reliable and reproducible that the data they generate, the measures of chemical relatedness, are now known as molecular clocks. Thus, comparative studies, like biogeographical and fossil studies, measure change across time. We will later see that the study of genes also requires thinking across time and that one of the keys to understanding genes is to bear in mind that they function and have meaning only in a time continuum. The failure to realize this property of genes is one of the great sources of confusion in the discussions of genes that appear in the popular literature.

24

Before turning our attention more fully to genes, it is well worth our while to consider comparative studies in a little more detail. Not only have comparative studies figured prominently in the history of evolutionary thought, but they remain central to our understanding of evolution today.

One of Darwin's most compelling arguments that the diversity of life resulted from descent with modification was based on evidence marshaled from comparative embryology and anatomy. It was already known, for example, that vertebrate organisms share a basic plan of early embryological development from their respective fertilized eggs. Thus, an untrained person, if shown comparably early embryos of diverse vertebrates, could only guess at their identities. This is illustrated below with fish, chicken, pig and human embryos. In such information, Darwin (and others) saw common descent. This embryological picture integrated comfortably with the fossil record and, particularly for Darwin, with his recently acquired knowledge of biogeography.

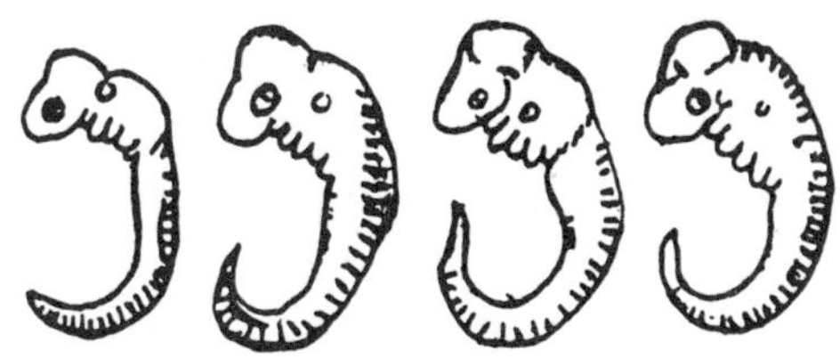

In addition to comparing processes of development, one can also compare the consequences or end-products of development. For example, as shown below for birds, whales and humans, the bones of the forelimbs of very diverse vertebrates are fully homologous to each other (the large bones of the human arm are labeled and their homologs indicated with ticks for the bird wing and whale flipper).

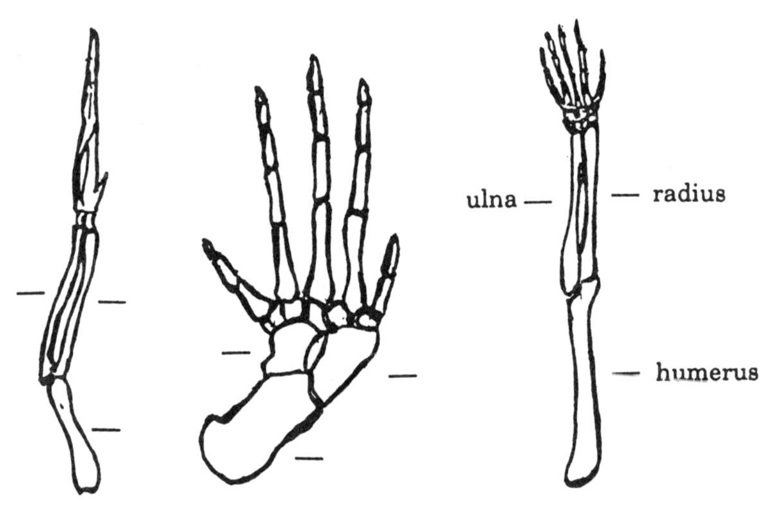

Birds are a qualified exception to the rule of homology in that their limbs differ by the loss of two "fingers" and by the fusion of certain other bones. Otherwise, they differ only by the relative sizes of the

26

bones. The limbs, and indeed the rest of the skeletons, of birds, whales, people and all other vertebrates are variations on a common theme.

From the perspective of evolution, the existence in diverse species of common embryological and anatomical themes is rational and parsimonious. Since Natural Selection is constrained to work with what is at hand, evolution can only build upon ancestral forms. The vertebrate forelimb, as a case in point, was invented once–it shows up in fossils hundreds of millions of years old–and Natural Selection has used that pattern to fashion each of the variants of that pattern we see today. While evolutionary thought embraces these developmental and structural limitations, any other model for the diversity of life must explain them away. If we had hired an engineering firm to design for us a flipper, a wing and an arm, and they came back with the same structure for each, we might say that, at best, they lacked imagination. At worst, we would say they lacked skill. In contrast, Natural Selection simply lacked alternatives.

The power of comparative analyses is evident in even the cursory glimpse of vertebrate embryology and anatomy we have indulged ourselves here. However, the full range of the comparative approach wasn't available until the past couple of decades. A few additional words about comparative biochemistry will complete this part of our story.

The biochemical manifestation of common descent takes several forms. One of these is seen by comparing a biological molecule found in different species across some portion of the phylogenetic spectrum. The protein hemoglobin, mentioned earlier, is found throughout the vertebrate world and even in mollusks like sea slugs (as a point of reference, the more widely known snails are also mollusks). It is possible to make pure isolates of this protein and to determine the sequence of amino acids from which it is constructed (the nature of amino acids and their relationship to proteins and genes will be taken up later). When this is done for human hemoglobin ß (beta), which is made up of 146 amino acids, and compared to the cognate molecules from a variety of other organisms, the following pattern emerges. Hemoglobin ß from the gorilla differs by one amino acid in 146, that from the Rhesus monkey by eight, that from mouse by 27, that from chicken by 45, that from the lamprey (a primitive fish that appeared in the fossil record 425 million years ago) by 125 and that from the sea slug by 127. In other words, the greater the phylogenetic difference between two organisms, the greater the structural difference in cognate proteins. As we shall see, this biochemical measure of relatedness is actually a genetic measure (the amino acid sequence of a particular protein is encoded in a specific gene). In the case of hemoglobin, the gene encoding the protein in humans is closely related to the cognate gene in gorillas, more

28

distantly related to that in chickens and very distantly related to that in the lamprey.

This relationship of proteins to phylogeny, which fulfills a prediction of Darwinian evolution, holds for a wide variety of proteins. There is, however, a class of proteins that is virtually unchanged across the phylogenetic spectrum and thus seems to violate this prediction. These proteins are known to students of biology as the highly conserved proteins, and the logic of their conservation turns out to strengthen the phylogenetic case. We can see this logic by comparing the circumstances in which changeable and conserved proteins operate.

Hemoglobin, an example of a phylogenetically changeable protein, plays the same role in all the organisms in which it occurs, but the environments in which it plays this role are variable. The cells that carry the molecule, the tissues in which it is oxygenated, and the tissues to which it carries the oxygen differ from organism to organism, creating the opportunity to optimize differing hemoglobin functions in differing functional environments. Natural Selection fine-tunes the way a protein performs its function through alterations of the protein's configuration. Since protein configuration is a function of the protein's amino acid composition, fine-tuning of protein function across time will be seen as change of amino acid composition across time.

The hemoglobin molecule is a particularly good example of this phenomenon in that it varies not only across phylogenetic time but, in some species, also varies across developmental time within a single individual. Humans, for example, carry duplicate copies of genes encoding hemoglobin and utilize these genes differentially during the life cycle. *In utero,* where one set of conditions for oxygen delivery exists, the fetus manufactures and utilizes one form of hemoglobin (fetal hemoglobin). Shortly after birth, the gene encoding fetal hemoglobin is "turned off" and an alternative gene is "turned on." The result is that before birth a form of hemoglobin fine-tuned to fetal life is in use, but *post partum* the change is made to a different form of hemoglobin, fine-tuned to adult life. Thus, genes encoding hemoglobin molecules have evolved both within lineages and between lineages across the phylogenetic spectrum. The rationale of Natural Selection is the same in these disparate circumstances–optimization of function to fit variable environments.

While hemoglobin is a relatively changeable protein, a group of proteins called the cytochromes is evolutionarily more conservative. Cytochromes play crucial roles in biological energy capture and are quite ancient. Cytochrome *c*, for example, is found in all eukaryotic[2] cells, from mammals to trees to fungi, and even in more primitive prokaryotic cells like bacteria.

The rate of change in cytochrome *c* is about one-third that of hemoglobin. The table below shows the number of amino acid substitutions that separate human hemoglobin ß and cytochrome *c* from these same proteins as they occur in three other species.

	Hemoglobin ß	Cytochrome *c*
Human	–	–
Rhesus monkey	8	1
Chicken	45	13
Frog	67	18

In bacterial cells, cytochrome *c* is found in the cell membrane that separates these organisms from the external environment. Eukaryotic cytochrome *c* is also located in a membrane, but in this case the membrane of a subcellular inclusion called a mitochondrion. This location of cytochrome *c* is the key to its conservation. There is now incontrovertible evidence that mitochondria are derived from a bacterial symbiont within a eukaryotic cell (see, for example, Margulis, 1981 and any recent biology text such as Campbell, 1993). In other words, mitochondria are bacterial cells, adapted to survive within host eukaryotic cells. It follows that eukaryotic cytochrome *c* is bacterial in origin and that, in eukaryotic cells, it retains not just its function but also the site at which it performs this function–the bacterial (mitochondrial) membrane. Since cytochrome *c* is doing the same job in virtually the same environment, Natural Selection operates to leave it largely unchanged.

This evolutionary rationale–retaining a proven performer in a conserved function across eons of phylogenetic time––reaches its zenith in a set of proteins called histones. Histones function in the packaging of DNA in the nuclei of eukaryotic cells. Since this function is not specific to the source of DNA (i.e., to the DNA's "sequence" or information content), it can be carried out in an essentially identical fashion in all organisms. That is, a protein that works well in one organism will work equally well in another. It is thus comprehensible that the rate of change (amino acid substitution) in histones is about one one-hundredth that in hemoglobin ß. In vernacular argot, Mother Nature tends not to fix things that are not broken.

When comparative analysis is performed at the level of DNA rather than protein, it reveals two additional molecular manifestations of common descent. We will come back to these in a later chapter, following a description of DNA function.

32

3. Vitalism

The Ancient Origins of Strange Ideas About Life

Too few of us have developed any especial talent, or motivation, for the exercise of putting ourselves in another person's place, and then seeing the world from that person's perspective. We can exploit the modest talents we do have, however, for a brief thought-experiment involving the human transition from hunter-gather to farmer-builder.

The cultural and technological benefits that ultimately arose from this transition seem to impress us all and we celebrate culture and technology continuously. We are less attentive to the difficulties that also developed out of the transition. One such difficulty concerns the way we perceive our relationship to Nature. Hunter-gatherers—like our early human ancestors—live in relative harmony with Nature. This observation is deceptively simple. In fact, it is the manifestation of a profound truth. Humans are part of Nature. Tragically, most modern humans live in denial of this truth, perceiving themselves as outside of or above Nature.

The primary origin of this tragedy is easy to discover. The ancestral human condition of living in harmony with Nature was transformed by the act of creating permanent settlements. Permanent settlements are confrontations with Nature. If we simultaneously confront Nature, and we do confront

Nature, while living in denial that we are part of Nature, and we do deny this, we will remain unaware that modern human life contains a most peculiar element of assault upon itself. The urge to confront Nature necessarily comes full circle.

We can examine the merits of this construction by putting ourselves in the shoes of ancient peoples. Consider a band of such ancestors, say 50,000 years ago, living a hunter-gatherer lifestyle over some part of the African Rift Valley. Let us imagine what life might have looked like through their eyes.

To any given individual, the other members of the band would have loomed large. There would have been a premium on security in numbers, the sharing of labor and the fruits of labor. It is a lead pipe cinch that there was attachment, affection and appreciation of one another.

The world outside the band would have been seen very much in terms of resources—there was a store of knowledge about the identities and locations of plants with edible parts. There was also a store of knowledge about animals—both those that could be caught and consumed and those capable of returning the favor (thus the presumed security in numbers).

They would always have been mindful of water and tailor their movements so that a source was never beyond access. They would be watchful for outcrops that signaled sources of materials for their increasingly sophisticated stone technology. These nomads were keenly attuned to resources—a band that strayed too far from essential resources would simply perish. Such people as these would have had limited opportunities to collect and cultivate worries. Life may not always have been easy or free of peril, but we can safely guess that it was pretty straightforward.

If we skip forward in time to a community of ancestors somewhere in the Middle East about 5,000 years ago, the opportunities for collecting and cultivating worries would already have become the art form that still lingers with us today.

This 5,000-year-old community would have lived in a permanent settlement next to some source of water, since settlements did not, and still do not, occur at sites without fresh water. We will picture a settlement on the banks of a river. The commitment to living on the banks of a river was one of the early and common examples of a confrontation with Nature.

One form of this confrontation occurred when the river rose—as all rivers do sooner or later. The settlers we are observing could no longer retreat from the rising waters the way the hunter-gatherers had done. Their structures, livestock, crops and stash of seeds for next year's planting were now in the river's path. In the event of a flood, the bounty of the river became transformed into Nature's wrath and, instead of a harmonious retreat, the settlers were reduced to railing against or pleading with Nature to stop the destruction. Nature was seen as angry whereas, in fact, it was merely raining. We can be utterly confident that this scenario played itself out fifty centuries ago because we know with absolute certainty that it still plays itself out today.

In drought years, the river fell. Hunter-gatherers were free to follow it to its source if need be. But settlers, whether their crops are failing for lack of rain or from the inability to raise water from the shrunken river, could only plead with Nature to return to what they see as proper: average weather. With the advent of settlement, the phenomenon of fluctuation, as natural as the sunrise, became an attack on humanity. As remarkable as it seems, even today, life-sustaining fair weather is "good" weather while life-sustaining stormy weather is "bad" weather.

Humans have undergone similar changes in their relationship to other phenomena. A hunter-gatherer band 50,000 years ago would have experienced earthquakes from time to time. They might have huddled together and would surely have been puzzled. But at the end of such an episode, life would usually go on, largely unchanged.

Five thousand years ago, in sharp contrast, the survivors of earthquakes could easily have found themselves retrieving the bodies of family members or neighbors from the rubble of their homes. Moreover, if they have been in this settled condition for even just a few generations, they would have forgotten the art of moving on. They had become

36

entrapped by their settlement because it was all they knew.

It is one of history's great ironies that by confronting Nature and coming to see itself as outside of Nature, humanity simultaneously intensified the need to explain Nature. Pre-settlement humans would have heard noises in the night and were no doubt troubled by yesterday's earthquake or last night's dream. They would have pondered a child's question and mourned the death of a loved one. But in settling, humans received the apparent lesson that the outside world was angry and vindictive. As we noted above, this perception of confrontation with Nature's hostility remains with us today. It is clearly powerful and persuasive.

There are signs that humans don't really like confrontation. For one thing, we almost always go to great lengths to explain our part in a confrontation (we have colorful names like sociopath for exceptions to this rule). Explaining a confrontation requires a statement of the grievance against the foe and, therefore, a model of the foe's behavior. With Nature as the foe, humans needed a model for Nature.

The tragedy that unfolded as humans first set about the task of modeling Nature was virtually inevitable. On the one hand, the scientific method— the idea of designing experiments to test models—lay millennia in the future. Secondly, their ignorance was, for practical purposes, absolute. They had no knowledge of geology or the fossil record. They knew nothing about cosmology. They knew nothing about cells, proteins or DNA. Given their lack of both methodology and information, together with the misconception that they were outside of Nature, their model of Nature—no matter its final form—would have to be wrong.

The model that came to prevail in the West employs the ingenious device of transforming Nature from hostile foe to magical but conditional gift. Nature as hostile foe is an awkward model because it has the qualities of being indeterminate and unpredictable. In contrast, when Nature is modeled as magic, it is presumed to be predictable, with the caveat that the Magician has the option, as a disciplinary device, of taking away the predictability. When something goes wrong—say there's a flood or an earthquake—it can be taken as a sign of the Magician's displeasure.

Here, then, is a rationale that not only explains the exigencies of human existence, but couples them to a code of proper human behavior. If humans behave themselves, tranquillity prevails and they exercise dominion over Nature. By definition, according to this scheme, a breakdown of tranquillity is the wrath of the Magician, precipitated by ill-conceived behavior on the part of the recipients. This model seems to work. Following a calamity, a chastened people will notice the restoration of tranquillity (never minding that this would also have occurred had they remained unchastened). If we bear in mind that the men who designed this model had no real knowledge of the natural world, we should probably all agree that they were brilliant. It is a remarkable product.

However, in spite of its brilliance, there are two things wrong with the ancient model of Nature. In the first place, it employs magic, not only to explain Nature, but also to place humans outside of Nature. The infusion of magic into biological systems, in particular, goes by the name vitalism (or, in some contexts, animism). Ultimately, the central claim of the vitalistic view is that life follows different laws of physics and chemistry than those followed by other parts of the natural world. In fact, this claim is exactly wrong. Biological systems follow the same laws with the same rigor observed in the non-biological world.

The second problem with the ancient model is that each phenomenon it attempts to explain by magic—floods, earthquakes, pestilence, hordes of locusts, human consciousness, and the advent of life—are now explicable by knowledge-based systems. We understand floods to arise from chaotic patterns in jet streams and ocean currents, earthquakes from movements of tectonic plates, and plagues from the cyclical workings of biological rhythms as they affect microorganisms and swarming insects. Even human intellect is being brought into focus by the operation of human intellect itself. The present need is not for continuing superstition, but for continuing inquiry.

However, in spite of the great advances in our knowledge of our world, the vitalistic view continues to hold great sway over the human mind. It is unlikely that this influence doesn't cause us to misunderstand ourselves and our place in Nature. It is inconceivable that misunderstanding ourselves doesn't work to our detriment.

One would presume that all vestiges of vitalism would first disappear from the thinking of people trained in science. Even so, within the last few decades, vitalism has energized important segments of the scientific community. One remarkable, but ultimately harmless, reincarnation of vitalism began with the publication of a little monograph titled *What Is Life?* by Irwin Schrödinger (1944; the same Schrödinger of wave mechanics fame). As a refugee from war-torn Europe, a variety of circumstances conspired to pique his interest in biology and led him to ask not so much "what is life" as "what is a gene?"

In brief, Schrödinger posed the rhetorical question (paraphrased here): will the study of biology (genes) reveal new physical laws? He then proceeded to answer this question in the negative, and did so with what seems letter perfect clarity. That is, he unambiguously rejected the vitalistic proposition that special laws operate in biological systems.[3]

In the immediate post-war years, Schrödinger's book, together with the malaise attendant upon the war itself, influenced a number of physicists to turn

40

their talents to the study of biology. If we are to believe the chroniclers of this episode (see, for example, Stent, 1966), the impact of Schrödinger was this: the physicists-turned-biologists were entranced and agitated by the romantic notion that they might discover new physical laws operating in biology. In other words, they seized upon Schrödinger's rhetorical question and ignored his rejection of the vitalism it implied. One might begin to suspect that humans—even highly educated humans—carry with them the desire that life be motivated by special forces unique to life. Humans want life to be different. The alternative explanation, at least in this case, is to consider the unpleasant possibility that physicists do not read well.

Schrödinger's foray into biology, given the misinterpretation of his conclusions, emerged as a happy accident. His physicist disciples brought with them to the study of biology their extraordinary technical and analytical skills, and an enthusiasm buoyed by the romantic notion that biology was different. It may therefore seem paradoxical that, in spite of their attachment to the possibility of new laws awaiting discovery, they didn't also bring preconceived notions They may have been excited by the prospect of new laws but had made no intellectual commitment to what those laws might be. Thus, they did not suffer the impediment of having to remove commitments to false notions before they could recognize the truth. Their ensuing contributions to our understanding of biology are well documented.

The last possible hiding place for vitalism was removed from biology in 1953. That, of course, was the year that Watson and Crick published their model for the structure of DNA. It contains no mysterious chemical or physical properties. It is just a big, gorgeous molecule. It is amazing but not magic.

The approach that Watson and Crick took in their quest for the structure of DNA—a form of three-dimensional modeling—had previously been used by Linus Pauling to solve the secondary structure of protein molecules. Indeed, Pauling was also on the trail of DNA structure. His considerable intellect was already the stuff of legend, and the widespread presumption that he would eventually solve DNA kept the fires burning in the Watson-Crick camp.

Pauling was a physical chemist by training, Watson a biologist (with expertise in the biology of viruses that infect bacteria) and Crick a physicist. Among other things, this diversity reflects the influence of Schrödinger. There is no doubt that this convergence of interest among biologists, physicists and chemists played a central role in the phenomenal success of molecular biology that was to follow.

The key to this coming together of scientists of diverse backgrounds, we should always bear in mind, was the focus on questions about the gene: what is it made of, what does it look like, and how does it work? The idea of the gene was one they could all think about in terms of their own training. They could all design experiments to test their models for what genes might be and how they might work. Since they were interested in genes first and organisms later, they chose to study genes of the simplest known biological systems, those of bacteria and especially the viruses of bacteria. The resulting burst of activity, and the virtual explosion in our knowledge and understanding of the inner workings of biological systems, is one of the great intellectual leaps in the history of science.

It could begin to sound a little as if molecular biology was parented by non-biologists, but the history is not quite that simple. Consider the words of H. J. Muller, abrasive star student of T. H. Morgan's famous fly lab at Columbia University. In 1922, addressing himself to the recently discovered "d'Herelle bodies" (d'Herelle body is a classical name for a virus that infects a bacterium) Muller wrote:

On the other hand, if these d'Herelle bodies were really genes, fundamentally like our chromosome genes, they would give us an utterly new angle from which to attack the gene problem. They are filterable, to some extent isolable, can be handled in test tubes, and their properties, as shown by their effects on the bacteria, can then be studied after treatment. It would be very rash to call these bodies genes, and yet at present we must confess that there is no known distinction between the genes and them. Hence we cannot categorically deny that perhaps we may be able to grind genes in a mortar and cook them in a beaker after all. Must we geneticists become bacteriologists, physiological chemists and physicists,

It is clearly the case that the seeds of molecular biology had already formed by 1922. Trained in the light of Morgan's towering intellect, the question Muller was addressing was the core question—what is a gene? In 1944, Schrödinger, aware of the work with Drosophila, was asking—what is a gene? In 1953, Watson and Crick, familiar with the theoretical musings of Schrödinger, were asking—what is a gene? So we must recognize and acknowledge that there developed a continuity around this central question of biology and that science, like life, builds upon what has come before. Today's most brilliant biologist, had he or she lived a thousand years ago, would have been fundamentally ignorant of the natural world and any methodology to study it. In the absence of our heritage, it is not possible to address the central questions. There are truly few things more ludicrous than a strutting scientist.

If life is not distinguished from non-life through divine or magical characteristics, or through special laws of chemistry and physics, then vitalism should be a thing of the past. However, vitalism lives on in more subtle ways. Although the potential for life, as carried from generation to generation by genes, is acknowledged to be neither divine nor physically unique, it has nonetheless had bestowed upon it a personality flaw. In its latest incarnation,

44

vitalism has surfaced in the form of a claim that genes are selfish. Like the ideas of genes by magic, and genes free from the yoke of physical and chemical laws, the idea that genes are selfish cannot and does not work.

4. The Idea of the Gene

The realization that life's information is particulate, encoded in a form we've come to know as the gene, has been and remains one of the great guiding ideas in biology. By thinking about genes, biologists have been able to penetrate life's most difficult questions. There are three properties of genes that cause this to be so.

In the first place, as already noted, genes are the primary information describing life. The biological potential of any organism consists of receiving and expressing all the information stored in the form of the genes of that organism. You, for example, began life as an egg cell, itself the product of the expression of your mother's genes, fertilized by a sperm cell, itself a product of your father's genes. The cell that resulted from the combination of egg and sperm, called a zygote, contained two sets of human genes, one from your mother and one from your father. Each of these sets of genes is carried in the form of a set of chromosomes, again, of course, one set being from your mother and one from your father.

The egg, a product of genes, plus the two sets of genes within the egg, comprised the totality of the biological information defining your inherited potential. The manifestation of that potential then depended upon the quality of nourishment and nurturing with which that fertilized egg was treated. We will describe the nature of the information stored

46

in genes and the means by which it is expressed a little later.

In addition to being an information storage and retrieval system, genes are a system of information replication and transmission. We are all familiar with the time-honored observation that like begets like. This phenomenon is entirely gene-based. On the one hand, cats beget cats and people beget people because their respective genic constellations contain cat information and people information. The information stored in genes is capable of being transmitted from an adult generation to a new generation because genes can be replicated. The genes of a new generation of cats or people are replicates of the genes of the parent cats or people. Defined genetically, life consists of replicating genes of an existing generation, transmitting those copies to a new generation and then retrieving the information contained in those genes and expressing it in that new generation. Genes are copied, transmitted and expressed—copied, transmitted and expressed—copied transmitted and expressed through the ages.

The third property of genes is one that gives large numbers of people great difficulty. Genes are mutable. Any copy of a gene that you inherited from one of your parents you might well pass on to one of your offspring in an altered form. In other words, the adage that like begets like is an approximation—like, in fact, begets approximately like. As a consequence of this phenomenon, any population is highly variable. No two individuals are genetically identical (and this assertion does apply to "identical" twins, who are very approximately alike).

The process of copying the genetic material is accurate enough that, in the course of a human lifetime, no easily perceived changes are likely to occur in any population under observation. It certainly seems that like begets like, but it is an illusion. In the course of geological time, like tends not to beget like.

We are belaboring this point about genetic accuracy across generations for a reason. If our goal is to understand life, we must develop the habit of mind that life is not static or discontinuous—life only occurs in a dynamic continuum. Genes are life's travelers in the continuum—you and I do not get to go on, but our genes can. Understanding genes, like understanding life, can thus be accomplished only in the context of time. Our lives are today's expression of mutable information traveling through time.[4]

Given that genes are information that is both mutable and continuous across time—and life tends in the direction of increasing sophistication and is not degenerate—then genes must be a measure of what has been learned across time. We will later consider the possibility of meaning or purpose to life in the context of the learning represented by life.

Because of the mutability of genes, all populations are variable. The variable individuals in a population can be thought of as alternative experiments in adaptation to the environment—any individual that is not adapted to its environment cannot survive. The idea of adaptation to the environment is an old one, and we tend to repeat it as fixed and unchangeable, as if it were law that the best adapted individuals survive. However, adaptation to one's environment can be restated in language that is at once faithful to the original conception and yet changes our perspective in key ways. We will begin to move away from the construction that a surviving organism is well adapted—an essentially passive relationship of the organism to its environment— towards the construction that a surviving organism interprets its environment well—an essentially experimental relationship of the organism to its environment.

If an organism arises as an experimental interpretation of its environment, then Natural Selection must be a challenge to that interpretation. We can picture Natural Selection as the question: how well does this organism interpret the place in which it is trying to reside? In other words, how well does its information—its genetic content—describe its world to it? Over time, descriptions persist if they are accurate representations of the environment. Newly invented descriptions are prized if they improve upon an old description or describe something that is useful but had not been described before.

One consequence of the view that evolution proceeds by way of experimental interpretations of the environment is that Mother Nature has to be seen as a scientist, long having been talented and systematic at doing what human scientists have only recently learned to do. She constructs multiple models of the environment (variable individuals) and then attempts to disprove them (Natural Selection). Doing experiments designed to disprove models (i.e., interpretations) is considered by some to be the most powerful form of the scientific method (see Platt, 1964, for a provocative discussion on the relative merits of different approaches to science).

From the genetic perspective we will develop here, the study of life is the study of information storage in the form of genes, and the study of the expression of that information across the time and space that define organisms. Likewise, the study of evolution is focused on the transmission of altered genetic information across the time and space that define life.

With this overview of the three core properties of genes, and the roles played by genes, we can now begin to address ourselves to questions about their personality. Are genes selfish? In particular, we will need to know what property of genes contains the alleged selfishness. Is the property of being information storage selfish? Is it selfish to replicate, or is it selfish to mutate—or is the selfishness imagined to exist in some combination of these properties?

50

Our first task is to be sure we understand what is meant by *selfish*. Let us consider some gene we can call <u>A</u>. As a gene, <u>A</u> is information that provides some benefit at one or more points in the life of the organism in which <u>A</u> resides. Since selfishness is asserted to be a universal property of genes, the information represented by <u>A</u> and the identity of the organism in which <u>A</u> resides are of no concern. For example, <u>A</u> could represent human hemoglobin ß, a protein necessary for the transport of oxygen from our lungs to all other tissues. Alternatively, <u>A</u> could represent bovine histone H1, a protein required for proper packaging of chromosomes in cows. Further afield, <u>A</u> could represent Saccharomyces (yeast) adenlyate synthetase, an enzyme with an essential role in the energetics of the cell.

Now suppose that at some point in geological time, a variant of <u>A</u> arises by spontaneous mutation, the mechanism of which we will explore later. The population of organisms in which this mutational event occurs now contains two varieties of the gene <u>A</u>. If we continue to call the original by the name <u>A</u>, we can call the new version <u>A1</u>. Different versions of the same gene are called *alleles* of each other, a useful term we will continue to employ. Let us imagine further that individuals carrying <u>A1</u> are at an advantage over individuals carrying <u>A</u>. Since individuals with an advantage survive longer or leave more offspring, <u>A1</u> begins to replace <u>A</u> in the population. Of course, the replacement of <u>A</u> by <u>A1</u>

occurs over a period of generations. The relative frequency of $\underline{A1}$ is very low when $\underline{A1}$ first appears in the population. It is a little higher in the first generation after its appearance, higher yet in the second, and so on. This replacement of the old version of $\underline{A}$ with the new version is based upon the advantage the new copy affords the organism. Gene selfishness, as represented in the book entitled *The Selfish Gene* (Dawkins, 1976), is defined by this replacement act. That is, $\underline{A1}$ is described as behaving selfishly towards $\underline{A}$. Indeed, such replacement acts are described as universal and ruthless selfishness. Historically, they have usually been described as consequences of Natural Selection.

One might think that an assessment of something so important as the idea that genes are selfish would require a thorough understanding of the basis or mechanism of the selfishness. That is, we need to know how $\underline{A1}$ differs from $\underline{A}$ and how this difference translates into selfishness. However, *The Selfish Gene* does not address this question. Instead, we are presented with a rather daring redefinition of the gene. A gene is classically defined as a unit of function—the gene that encodes human hemoglobin ß, for example, encodes and expresses exactly that protein, neither more nor less. The selfish gene is redefined as a constellation of such functional units, a group of classical genes physically close to each other (i.e., in the same vicinity on one chromosome). Genes

52

close to each other on the same chromosome tend to be inherited together (they are said to show genetic linkage). About ten pages of text in *The Selfish Gene* are devoted to redefining a gene as a cluster of genes—it is clearly seen as important. Whether intentional or not, this redefinition is also a subterfuge. It avoids the question of mechanism.

Since *The Selfish Gene* doesn't inquire into the mechanism of the alleged selfishness, we shall have to do it ourselves. And here is the rub—the variation seen by Natural Selection is not multi-genic at all— it is sub-genic. The variation that distinguishes two versions of the same gene occurs within the gene and affects only a part of it. By redefining a gene as a cluster of genes, attention is drawn away from the sub-genic nature of variation. We can illustrate how this muddies the waters by way of a little painless dabbling in molecular genetics.

The language of life, at the level of information storage in DNA, is written with just four "letters." These letters consist of two very similar molecules, adenine (A) and guanine (G), plus two other molecules, different from A and G but quite like each other, thymine (T) and cytosine (C; see Appendix 1). Adenine, guanine, thymine and cytosine are a class of molecules called nucleotides and exist in specific pairs in the two strands of a DNA double helix. Adenine is always paired with thymine, and guanine is always paired with cytosine. Thus, if one stand of a DNA molecule contains the sequence AGTCAGTC, the other strand will contain the sequence TCAGTCAG. Each strand is said to be the complement of, or to be complementary to, the other. The two strands taken together will then have the sequence:

AGTCAGTC
TCAGTCAG

If this short sequence were part of a gene, which typically consists of a thousand or more pairs of nucleotides, the information contained in the sequence would be read from just one of the two strands in non-overlapping sets of three (the genetic code is therefore said to be triplet). If the above sequence were read from the bottom strand, left to right, we would have:

TCA•GTC•AG•••••

Notice that there are four possibilities for the first letter of a triplet (A, G, T or C), the same four possibilities for the second letter and for the third. Therefore, there are 4x4x4=64 possible triplet words. All of life's information is written in these 64 words. Every gene is a sentence comprised of some sequence of these words. This brief description of genetic information will be sufficient for present purposes. It will be treated in greater detail in a subsequent chapter.

We now return to the example of gene <u>A</u> and the new allele we called <u>A</u>1. One of the more

54

common ways that mutation can cause the change of a gene $\underline{A}$ to an allelic form such as $\underline{A1,}$ is by changing one of the letters in one of the words, thus yielding a new word and therefore a new sentence with similar but altered information. Suppose the original gene $\underline{A}$ had the sequence:

GCG
CGC

as the twentieth word of a sentence 300 words long (300 words or 900 letters is a more or less common size for the coding part of a gene). We will stipulate that the word is read as CGC–i.e., read left to right from the bottom strand. Now suppose $\underline{A1}$ has, at position twenty, the sequence:

ACG
TGC

in place of the original. The new word, which is still read left to right from the bottom strand, is TGC. The $\underline{A1}$ version of the gene differs from $\underline{A}$ by a single letter (this is technically called a base pair substitution mutation). If we compare the new word to the old word, we see that the difference is a change to T from C. The figure below shows the structural formulae for T and C. One can quickly see that the differences between the molecules are less than startling and, neither biologically nor chemically, do they suggest to us any notion of selfishness (C = carbon, H = hydrogen, N = nitrogen, O = oxygen).

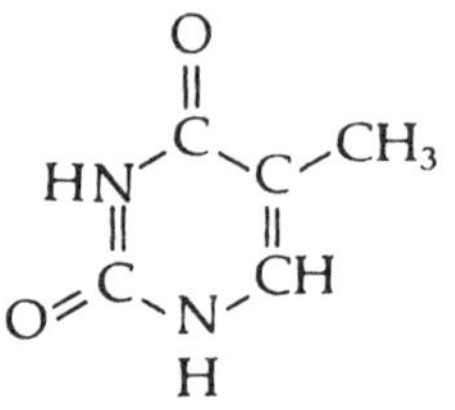

THE GENETIC LETTER T 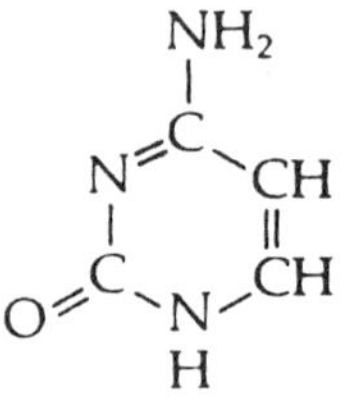   THE GENETIC LETTER C

In this example, the legitimacy of which has been confirmed many times over, the replacement of A by its allele A1 is in actuality the replacement of a few atoms by a few different atoms. One can see that information has changed, but it is less easy to see how this change of one letter among nine hundred letters yields a selfish product. Somehow, the idea of selfishness seems bigger than this.

There is, however, an even greater difficulty with the practice of calling changes such as that of A to A1 selfish. Although there are genes in which the word CGC has been changed to TGC, there are other genes, somewhere in the biosphere, in which an improved version arose as the consequence of the opposite change, from TGC to CGC. In other words, the utility of a change in a gene is a function of the context in which that change occurs–the utility depends upon the gene itself. *The utility of a change in a gene is dependent upon that part of the gene that did not change. Natural Selection sees the change within the*

56

context of the rest of the information of the gene sentence. We say this with absolute certainty.

If the effectiveness of a change in a gene is determined by the context in which that change occurs, our focus must shift from that which has changed to that which has remained the same—i.e., to the context itself. Since the context of the change is the rest of the gene, a one-word change in a gene that is 300 words long yields a new version of that gene in which 299 of the 300 words are identical to those in the old version. If the one word in 300 that did change makes the whole of the information more useful, so that the changed gene goes on to replace the original, the original gene might "think" it did all right after all. At the level of its letters, it is 899/900 preserved, and since the gene is more robust than before, the 899 preserved letters are more robust than before. The original version of the gene, the alleged victim of ruthless selfishness, is actually quite "happy." If it has been treated selfishly, it is quite unaware of it.

Perhaps it would be more fruitful to look for signs of selfishness at the next level of gene function— that of expressing its stored information. It is, after all, the expressed (as opposed to the stored or latent) information that Natural Selection surveys. Therefore, let us examine what it means for a gene to be expressed.

There are four basic sorts of information storage carried out by DNA. Most generally, when we refer to a gene, we have in mind a length of DNA with precisely defined ends such that the words lying between those ends encode a specific protein (like the hemoglobin, histone and adenylate cyclase proteins mentioned above). The production of proteins is accomplished by translating the genetic language into the protein language.

The words in the protein language are molecules known as amino acids. The protein dictionary contains twenty of these amino acid words. One genetic word, a triplet of nucleotides, is translated into one protein word, an amino acid. Two adjacent triplets in DNA encode two adjacent amino acids in the protein product. Since there are twenty amino acids, there are 400 possible sequences of two amino acids (twenty possibilities for the first amino acid times twenty possibilities for the second). We asserted above that a more or less typical gene is about 300 triplets long. It therefore encodes a protein that is 300 amino acids long. There are approximately one hundred thousand billion billion billion possible proteins of this length (20^{300}). Humans, in contrast, have about 100,000 genes and thus produce about 100,000 proteins. Clearly, Mother Nature has just begun to explore the possibilities.

Earlier, we considered the genetic word CGC and a variant, TGC, at position 20 of a genetic sentence. When translated into a protein sentence, CGC turns out to represent the amino acid alanine. (A word of explanation is in order here. If you were to look at a table of the genetic code, you would find a *codon*, GCG rather than a *word*, CGC, representing alanine. Codons are intermediaries in the translation process. We are here using the designation *word* to represent what is actually stored as DNA information.) The word TGC represents the amino acid threonine. Alanine and threonine are shown below—again with their differences easily discerned—and, like the nucleotides, these molecules fail to communicate to us any signs of their alleged selfishness.

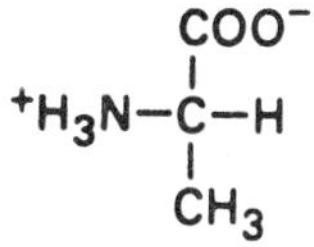

$$^+H_3N-\underset{\underset{CH_3}{|}}{\overset{\overset{COO^-}{|}}{C}}-H$$

$$^+H_3N-\underset{\underset{\underset{CH_3}{|}}{\overset{|}{H-C-OH}}}{\overset{\overset{COO^-}{|}}{C}}-H$$

THE PROTEIN WORD
ALANINE

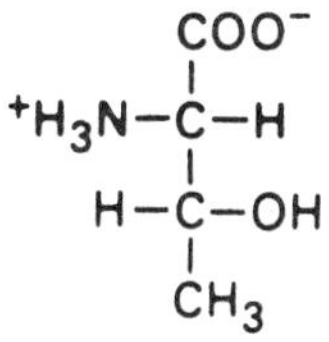

THE PROTEIN WORD
THREONINE

If the specific example we've used here for illustration, T replacing C in DNA, threonine replacing alanine in protein, were simply anecdotal, it would be little more than a curiosity. However, this example is entirely representative and the conclusions to be drawn from it are general conclusions. Although more complex mutational events do occur, they do not violate these general conclusions. In fact they confirm and reinforce these conclusions which we recapitulate here.

•Inherited biological variation is produced by mutation, specific chemical alterations at the level of DNA. There are no mysterious forces or special physical or chemical laws at work.

•The biological consequences of a specific alteration, such as a C to T transition, depend upon the local environment or context in which it occurs. The context is the rest of the gene. There is no mechanism by which a gene, altered by mutation, can insinuate itself into the community of genes by virtue of its alleged selfishness. The first thing a new genetic variant has to do, figuratively, is ask permission. "Is it OK for me to be here?" A new variant of a gene does not assert itself. It asks. Asking permission is not generally considered a selfish act.

Indeed, the selfish gene idea is incompatible with Natural Selection. Each generation, genes are submitted to the natural world in the form of new individuals. Mother Nature scrutinizes these offerings and decides upon their suitability. One might even go so far as to suggest that this submission to scrutiny is more easily understood as a selfless than a selfish act. But genes simply do not have the power to decide upon this submission to scrutiny. They are utterly and absolutely helpless to do otherwise. Genes submit.

To this point, we have framed the discussion about whether genes have personality in terms of the verified properties of genes. When we focus on these properties–which can be paraphrased as capacity to act as information storage, capacity to vary (mutability) and submission to scrutiny (transmission into a new generation)—the idea that genes are selfish does nothing to advance our understanding of these properties of the gene. Our understanding of Natural Selection, in contrast, is stood on its head—genes driving it, rather than it allowing them.

We can carry the critique of gene selfishness to a level of biological organization beyond the chemistry of genes and proteins. In fact, most of the evidence that has been marshaled in support of the idea of gene selfishness comes not from a contemplation of genes, but from the study of animal behavior—the leading advocates of the selfish gene idea are students of animal behavior. An encapsulated version of their rationale goes something like this. The size, shape, habitat preferences and behavior of any given animal reflect the expression of all its genes (its potentials are genetic). Some animal behaviors may be labeled selfish. Therefore, the genes which create the potential for this selfish behavior are selfish. Since the latter genes work in concert with the rest of the genes that define the potentials of the organism, all genes are selfish.

The studies that have led to the creation of this rationale are diverse, ranging from territoriality in mammals to sex ratios in ants. It may at first seem odd that we would seek guidance on important biological questions by asking questions of something like ants, but the precedents for this approach are many and rich. For example, as mentioned earlier, the emergence of molecular biology is intimately related to the adoption of bacterial viruses as objects of study. If you have even a passing familiarity with biology, you have probably heard of *Drosophila melanogaster* and its widespread use for investigations of genetic principles. Similarly, you are apt to have heard of laboratory mice and rats and their use for studies of mammalian immune response. When we use ants, fruit flies, mice and rats, we refer to them as model systems. It is important to understand that studies of model systems have yielded most of what we now know about biology, including our own.

One of the more remarkable facts of ant biology is the mechanism by which their sex determination occurs. Individuals that arise from an egg that has been fertilized by a sperm develop as females. In other words, females have two sets of chromosomes, one from their queen mother and one from their father. Individuals with two sets of chromosomes are called diploid.

In contrast, unfertilized ant eggs develop as males (unfertilized eggs in the vast majority of organisms, including humans, do not develop at all). A male, then, has a single set of chromosomes inherited from the queen. Individuals with a single

62

set of chromosomes are called haploid. Haploid male ants have no father.

Now we are going to do some thinking about numbers. Out of deference to anyone who might not care for thinking about numbers, it is first necessary to show that this is an interesting thing to do. Queen ants, as we have seen, are capable of laying eggs that are either fertilized (these will become daughters) or unfertilized (these will become sons). All of the males will develop as reproductives. (They are sexually active. In fact, that is about all they do.) On the other hand, depending upon their treatment during development from egg to adult, females may become sterile workers or fertile queens. (This is the ideal case. Not all ant species maintain an absolute distinction between workers and queens.) In principle, since development as a queen depends upon the treatment of fertilized eggs, and the treatment is meted out by workers, the number of developing queens in a colony is a function of worker behavior. The sex ratio in a brood, then, is the combined outcome of embryos (larvae) developing from unfertilized eggs ("controlled" by the queen) and the number of diploid embryos given special, queen producing, treatment by workers. Therefore, if workers can count, it is within their power to adjust the sex ratio as they see fit.

It is precisely such a counting behavior that some students of animal behavior have proposed and upon which *The Selfish Gene* seizes. Their proposal takes the additional step of interpreting the phrase "as they see fit." The worker ants, according to this interpretation, see fit to adjust the sex ratio in a manner that maximizes the transmission of their genes (the workers' genes) to the next generation, and they do this as an act of selfishness. The model that emerges, which we will now review, is at first glance ingenious and mathematically elegant. It is also completely wrong.

Fortunately, the mathematics of this model are simple enough that I, a non-mathematician, can explain it and anyone, including other non-mathematicians, can fully comprehend it. We begin with a queen who is diploid and therefore has two copies of some gene a. We name these two copies a1 and a2 (i.e., her genotype or genetic constitution is a1a2). She mates with a male who has a single copy of gene a which we will call a3. Their progeny will be females of constitution a1a3 and a2a3 in equal numbers. That is, a female will be equally likely to have inherited a1 or a2 from her mother but can only inherit a3 from her father. The male progeny will be equal numbers of a1 and a2 individuals.

Out of this brood emerges a worker female who will tend her younger sisters and brothers. Imagine that this particular worker is a1a3. Her sisters are a1a3 (i.e., identical to her) and a1a2 (i.e., one-half like her). Thus, her average relatedness to her sisters is 3/4. Her brothers are either a1 or a2. Her a1 brothers are half like her and her a2 brothers

64

are unrelated. Thus, on average, her relatedness to her brothers is 1/4. Remarkably, she is three times more closely related to her sisters than to her brothers. I will ask you to accept the assertion that this relationship is true for all genes and, therefore, true for individuals.

The next step in the model is more daring. The theorists of the selfish gene argue that it is in the genetic interest of female workers to produce three times as many queens as males, because they are three times more closely related (technically, they argue that the workers will produce three times more female than male mass, but the distinction does not affect us).

One of the key publications in support of this model is a 1976 paper (Trivers and Hare) reporting measurements of investment in male and female reproductives in haplo-diploid species. They present an impressive array of data indicating a rather nice fit of observations to the 3:1 prediction of the model. In other words, their results seem to demonstrate that female workers count developing queens and males and favor queens with three times as much attention.

This would stand as a remarkable finding if only it were true. However, any euphoria felt by proponents of selfish genes was destined to be short-lived. Little more than a year later, there followed a paper (Alexander and Sherman, 1977) that not only raised questions about aspects of theoretical expectations, but also raised serious objections about the data themselves. The seriousness of this challenge is acknowledged in an "endnote" in the 1989 edition of *The Selfish Gene.* However, the author does not recant. Instead, he expresses regret that such a pretty idea as the 3:1 investment ratio might not be true after all.

The criticism I will develop here of the three queens to one male prediction is more direct. I will argue below that this model, and the experiments done to test it, are full of egregious logical and methodological flaws.

The Mating Bottleneck. One of the things upon which we all can agree is that, in sexually reproducing species like ants, flies and humans, each act of sexual reproduction requires a male and a female (we ignore hermaphrodites here). A worker ant, if she really has the ability to measure genetic relatedness among her brothers and sisters, would need to apply that ability to her real and not her imagined problem. Her real problem is this:

1.   Her genetic legacy, if she actually has
     one, is fundamentally dependent upon the
     reproductive success of her queen sister.
2.   The reproductive success of her queen sister
     is absolutely dependent upon becoming
     inseminated.
3.   Insemination of the queen sister requires the
     presence of a male.

66

At this particular moment of biological truth, an act that enables the next generation, the female is of course absolutely necessary. What the selfish gene idea fails to keep in focus is that the male is also absolutely necessary. At this particular moment of biological truth, the sex ratio is 1:1. If we generalize this realization across all matings, the effective sex ratio in ants is 1:1, and it becomes quite unclear what good would have been done by all that theoretical attention to queens. If a worker's genetic legacy is tied to the success of her queen sister, that worker had better be sure there's a male around to service her queen sister. This can be stated in another way: no matter how much attention a worker lavishes upon her queen sister, that queen sister will hit the mating bottleneck and she must have a mate.

The critical point of the 1:1 sex ratio is that, in the absence of either the female or the male, the process fails. The lineage in which this occurs will become extinct. It is inescapable that both the female and the male are absolutely necessary and, therefore, absolutely equal. The selfish gene model thus contains the curious condition that one absolute equal be more absolutely equal than another absolute equal. (The equal necessity of males and females cannot be avoided by invoking males from another, external source since such excess males would have to come from a population operating by a different set of rules than that operating in the population we have under consideration. The counting that is claimed to occur in haplo-diploid species cannot be meaningful if it is not general.)

We also see, in this admittedly clever model for the control of sex ratio in ants, a problem we saw when examining the selfish gene idea at the level of molecules. The assertion that workers are controlling the genetic constitution of the succeeding generation flies in the face of Natural Selection. What survives in succeeding generations will be determined by the soundness of the individuals in that generation. The determination of soundness is not the province of workers in the present generation, but of Natural Selection in the succeeding generation. Once again, the idea of the selfish gene does not comport well with Darwinian biology.

<u>The Continuity Paradox.</u> The selfish gene model at first makes mathematical sense if we limit our attention to gene transmission from one generation to the next. However, if we extend the examination to multiple generations and think about genes in the continuum in which they actually exist, a paradox emerges. We will now show that any apparent genetic advantage that a queen can enjoy in perpetuity can only express itself through sons. In this event, a worker who discriminates against brothers is actually working against the genetic advantage the selfish gene theorists claim she is working for.

We can illustrate this phenomenon with the same mating scheme we used earlier. That began with a female designated <u>a1a2</u> and a male designated <u>a3</u>. Their offspring were <u>a1a3</u> and <u>a2a3</u> females plus <u>a1</u> and <u>a2</u> males. Equal numbers of the <u>a1a3</u> and <u>a2a3</u> females will become queens. Their offspring are shown in the table below, where a_m is a copy of <u>a</u> from any male (that is, it could be <u>a1</u>, <u>a2</u> or a copy of <u>a</u> from some other source, say, <u>a4</u>).

PARENTAL GENERATION	1ST GENERATION OFFSPRING	2ND GENERATION OFFSPRING OF AN:	
		a1a3 Queen	a2a3 Queen
$a1a2$	$a1a3$	$a1a_m$	$a2a_m$
	$a2a3$	$a3a_m$	$a3a_m$
$a3$	$a1$	$a1$	$a2$
	$a2$	$a3$	$a3$

According to the argument based on the selfish gene model, female workers of the first generation (the second column in the table) will favor their sisters over their brothers. This produces what must be an unintended result. Half of the genes they are coddling came from their mother, but the other half came from their father. They are rewarding their father equally with their mother. *Meanwhile, if they downplay the importance of their brothers, they are handicapping their mother, who contributed all of the* genes *to those brothers.*

If the females of the second generation (third and fourth columns) also indulge their sisters, they, too, are rewarding their fathers. In other words, the queens of the first generation, who were supposedly favored by their worker sisters, produce nieces of those workers who are giving as much attention to a̲m̲ from any male as to the copies of a̲ that came from their mother. *The nieces show no gratitude at all.*

In the final analysis, Natural Selection would be unable to see that worker sisters are favoring queen sisters if those same workers are simultaneously favoring their fathers. When this scheme is viewed across time, the males are doing splendidly and sister felicity to sisters simply makes no biological or evolutionary sense. This, you will recall, is exactly the conclusion that followed from the bottleneck phenomenon.

The failure to view gene transmission across time is a common one, afflicting a variety of people. By imposing stasis on a system that operates in a continuum, one can sometimes imagine seeing what one wants to see. In the end, though, we need to see things the way they actually are. As regards the genes of an ant, the issue is not where they came from, but how well they function.

Meanwhile, we briefly turn our attention to the second manner of problem affecting the selfish gene idea—the problem of methodology. We have been reviewing the claim that workers in haplo-diploid species, who are three times more closely related to their queen sisters than to their brothers, would therefore be expected to devote themselves to the

70

nurturing of three times as many sisters or three times as much sister mass. We have simply called it sex ratio. We have shown that the prediction has no basis in genetics. We will now show that the prediction itself cannot be interpreted and is thus empty of meaning.

The first manifestation of a methodological problem is that the prediction and the experiments done to test it, focus on the variable of genetic relatedness while simultaneously ignoring a second variable—one that has all the subtlety of a blow from a sledgehammer. The queens are diploid: each of their cells has two sets of chromosomes, while the males are haploid: each of their cells has but one set of chromosomes. Haploidy versus diploidy, regardless of sex, is itself a variable. Failing to see this variable has devastating consequences. Any cell biologist will tell you that one of Mother Nature's favorite ways of adjusting the size of cells is by adjusting the number of chromosome sets within cells. More chromosome sets equals greater cell size. To a first approximation, cell size (volume) is proportional to the number of chromosome sets within the cell.

One of the truly remarkable examples of this phenomenon occurs in certain larval tissues of Dipterans (flies) like Drosophila. Drosophila salivary glands contain cells with as many as a thousand copies of the chromosome complement. (The copies of each chromosome are aligned together in perfect register so that they have the appearance of single giant chromosomes). The cells containing these large numbers of chromosomes are themselves enormous.

This relationship of cell size to chromosome content leads to the prediction that haploid males would be smaller than diploid females, not because workers pay less attention to them, but because of the size of their cells. If it were found that a brood contained less male mass than queen mass (remembering that this result is unconfirmed), it cannot be interpreted. The methodology, simply weighing the ants, cannot distinguish between the behavior model (solicitous sisters) and the cell physiology model (congenital feebleness of males).

Haploid males are also susceptible to a second possible effect on their size. Since they have only one copy of each gene, any copy containing sub-optimal information will be directly detectable in its bearer. This might be lethal to the bearer male, thus reducing the number of males, or be detrimental to its bearer, thus having the potential to further reduce his size.

Mother Nature has at least two options at her disposal to increase the robustness of her haploid males. One option is to increase the rate of expression of the single set of genes in males—in effect to make each gene "work" as hard as if it were two copies of the gene. This type of adjustment is known to affect the expression of genes on the sex chromosomes in animals with an XY sex determination system. In Drosophila, the single X chromosome in males is expressed at a level that equals the total expression of

72

the two X chromosomes in females. This adjustment is known as dosage compensation.

A second possibility is to adjust the developmental program so that a male would consist of more cells than a female—making up in numbers of cells what his cells lack in size. There is precedent for this occurrence in certain newts.

In any event, the facile conclusion that male mass should be a function of worker behavior ignores a fundamental relationship of cell mass to chromosome content. Before attempting studies of the behavioral determination of mass, one is compelled to verify the basal mass. Do males and females have the same size and the same probability of survival if given the same treatment? This is called doing the control.

There is an additional, and purely anecdotal, reason for skepticism about the relationship between sisters and sex ratio in haplo-diploid species. Honeybees, *Apis melifera*, like ants, have haploid males, diploid females, and queen production controlled by female workers. As an amateur beekeeper for many years, one of the things I have noticed about honeybees is that the haploid males are huge and numerous. My impression is that a hive with a few developing queens has dozens to hundreds of drones—the colorful name for males—and that their mass vastly exceeds that of queens. If relative sexual mass is actually an interesting thing to study, one could do it in bees, which are much more tractable than ants.

A second methodological problem with the claim of a behavioral basis for perceived differences in male and female mass goes right to the heart of what genes are, how they do what they do, and how people trained in genetics study them. Like most people who only dabble in genetics, the advocates of the selfish gene idea have elaborate ideas about genes but fail to follow up those claims by actually doing genetic analysis (certain sociologists, psychologists, and even an occasional electrical engineer have made incredible spectacles of themselves in this fashion). Such people make claims that some biological variation or other is the result of the action of a gene or genes but ignore the most powerful tool for validating their claims. That tool is the simple expedient of identifying the genes responsible. In the case of the claim that female ants adjust sex ratio, we demand the following point of scientific rigor: show us the genes responsible for this claimed behavior. If you show us the genes involved, we have to believe you.

With this, we have arrived at the doorstep of genetic analysis, one of the most effective tools in the study of biological phenomena. It is also relatively easy to understand. There is, however, a step we have to negotiate that might at first seem to have come from Lewis Carroll. This follows from the fact that the initial stages in genetic analysis do not focus

74

on what the gene of interest normally does. Instead, the focus is on what occurs when the gene fails to do what it normally does. One proceeds by finding mutant forms of a gene and then sets out to discover the gene's function by analyzing what happens when the gene isn't doing it. If we can discern what is wrong under the influence of a mutant form of a gene, we can infer what is right under the influence of the normal form. Genetic analysis begins with the study of the "un-gene" to gain insight into the normal function.

We can highlight the major features of this methodology by way of a review of a gene so widely known that it may indeed be famous–the <u>white</u> gene in Drosophila. We begin with an overview of the biology and genetics of this gene.

The <u>white</u> gene is located on the X chromosome, so that females have two copies while males have but one (males have a single X chromosome and a Y chromosome which has no copy of <u>white</u> on it). A Drosophila female with two non-mutant copies of the gene has the red eye color that is the normal or wild-type condition for these fruit flies. We refer to her as homozygous and symbolize her genotype as $\underline{w}^+/\underline{w}^+$. If she has one normal copy and one mutant copy (she is $\underline{w}^+/\underline{w}$ or heterozygous) she nonetheless has red eyes. We say that $\underline{w}^+$ is dominant to $\underline{w}$. In other words, one normal copy of the information stored in this gene is sufficient to allow the cells of the Drosophila eye to develop their red coloration. In contrast, a female with two mutant copies of the gene (she is $\underline{w}/\underline{w}$) has white eyes.

The situation in males is different. Since a male inherits his Y chromosome from his father and his X from his mother, sons of $\underline{w}^+/\underline{w}^+$ females will all have red eyes (they are all $\underline{w}^+/Y$). A white-eyed female (she is $\underline{w}/\underline{w}$) will have all white-eyed sons. However, a red-eyed female who is $\underline{w}^+/\underline{w}$ will have a mixed brood of sons. Half will be red-eyed ($\underline{w}^+/Y$) while half will be white-eyed ($\underline{w}/Y$).

The latter female is of particular interest to us. Her production of equal numbers of red-eyed and white-eyed sons is one of the pivotal observations in biology. This observation is known formally as Mendel's first law. In more operational language, it is known as the segregation of members of a gene pair. It is implicit that this behavior occurs only during a special form of cell division—meiosis—that is unique to gamete production. The two members of the gene pair are packaged with equal frequency into the gametes. Thus, in the present example, the $\underline{w}^+/\underline{w}$ female produces equal numbers of eggs with $\underline{w}^+$ and $\underline{w}$ and, therefore, equal numbers of sons with red and white eyes. The mechanics of this chromosome behavior in meiotic cell division are outlined in Appendix 2.

With a few moments' reflection, one sees that something very special has happened here. In short order, we have been able to identify a gene and learn something about the information it stores. Both of

76

these findings, the very existence of the gene and the nature of the role it plays in the economy of the organism, were made possible by discovery and study of a mutant copy of the gene. Before the w allele was found, we had no way of knowing the white gene was there. If all females were w^+/w^+ and all males were w^+/Y, we would only know that these flies had red eyes. We would not know why their eyes were red.

Possession of a mutant copy of a gene allows us to discover a third thing about that gene. Through a method called gene mapping (Briefly described in Appendix 2), we can also learn its physical location. Now the mutant has told us three things: (1) the existence of the gene, (2) something about the role of the gene and (3) where to find it if we want to study it further—for example, to learn how it expresses that function. Molecular biology begins to beckon.

Now we can return to the idea that worker females in haplo-diploid species "count" the queens and males among their siblings and thus are empowered to favor their more closely related queen sisters over their brothers. The first step in a test of this idea would be to determine what the ratio of queens to males actually is. If that ratio proved to be 3:1, it would be regarded as consistent with the selfish gene prediction that workers count queens and males. As we have already seen, it cannot be taken as evidence for this proposition, since there are competing explanations. Notice that the determination of the ratio of queens to males is merely a preparatory step in genetic analysis. The advocates of the selfish gene model took it to be the answer.

The next step in the analysis is the actual test of the idea. This would be accomplished by searching for mutations that obliterate or otherwise alter the counting mechanism. That is, one would look for variants that no longer maintain the 3:1 ratio (if that were the ratio actually determined in the first step above). The rationale for this step is straightforward. If haplo-diploid species have the capacity to assess relatedness or count queens versus brothers, the potential for that capacity must be transmitted from generation to generation in the form of genetic information. It would thus be possible to find mutations in the specific genes that contain this information such that the capacity to count is lost or otherwise modified. Furthermore, the capacity to count would segregate from the incapacity as $\underline{w}^+$ segregates from $\underline{w}$ (the normal and mutant alleles would follow Mendel's first law). Moreover, the mutant would only express itself in females, since this is where the claimed behavior occurs. The genotype of males would be irrelevant to the functioning of this gene. Notice especially that in addressing this question with genetic analysis, we graduate from the weak scientific criterion of correlation (degree of genetic relatedness correlated with sex ratio) to the powerful criterion of cause and effect (the

78

identification of a gene or genes that provide the potential for the behavior).

If a mutation affecting sex ratio were found, we would give it a name. For example, it could be called <u>ratio</u> <u>distorter</u> and might be symbolized <u>rd</u>. It may already have occurred to you, when we discussed the <u>white</u> locus, that we do not necessarily name a gene after its function. Instead, we usually name genes after the effect of mutant copies.[5] This is because it was the mutant copy that alerted us to the presence of the gene in the first place. It's a little like naming a phenomenon in honor of its discoverer.

We might summarize this critique of the selfish gene idea this way: the proponents of the idea talk about genes but do not think about genes. If we actually focus on the chemical basis of genetic variation—it is ultimately this variation that must provide the basis of the proposed selfishness—it is difficult to visualize selfish interest. What one does see is a change in information content. Furthermore, the characterization of this information as selfish suggests that it imposes itself upon Natural Selection. This view conflicts sharply with the classical view that such information changes must submit (helplessly) to the scrutiny of Natural Selection. The alternatives are stark. Either selfish genes select themselves in a scheme of evolution by genetic assertion or helpless genes run the gauntlet of Natural Selection.

When we change our focus from the level of the gene to the level of the organism, the utility of the selfish gene idea fares no better. It has induced its proponents to propose, for example, the paradox that there is a biological advantage in producing more female than male reproductives in order to achieve a 1:1 sex ratio.

It is possible to assert, then, the following propositions regarding the selfish gene model.

1. The idea is grounded in errors, among them mistaking a 1:1 sex ratio for a 3:1 sex ratio.
2. The idea is anti-Darwinian. It invests within a gene the power to select itself through its own imposition on Nature, rather than being submitted passively to the scrutiny of Nature.
3. The idea is vitalistic—it invests purpose in the gene—the purpose of subduing inferior alleles. In the real world, genes replace less favorable alleles through the beneficence of Natural Selection. Genes do not dictate their terms to Mother Nature.

The initial appeal of the idea of gene selfishness is readily identified—it follows from a philosophical antecedent often embraced with an almost religious fervor. This antecedent is the thought that Natural Selection concerns itself with individuals. It is to the logical impossibility of this proposition that we must now turn.

5. Group Selection

It Takes Two to Entangle[6]

On a typical University campus, biology is one of the most popular areas of study. Given this popularity, it comes as no surprise that some of the courses in the curriculum are themselves popular. Genetics, however, is seldom in this category. It is usually seen as difficult and too time consuming, especially because it requires problem solving, and the problems may seem to border on the incomprehensible.

The perception that genetics problems are difficult is a little odd. The required computational skills—simple arithmetic and high school algebra—cannot be the issue. Perhaps the major difficulty is that the subject is simply a little different. The minimal experiment in genetics requires two parents and their offspring. A typical experiment in genetics may require tracking multiple individuals through three or more generations. In other words, genetics is not done by focusing on a static individual but by focusing on dynamic populations, groups or families of individuals. People tend to develop a block or to begin daydreaming when confronted with these circumstances.

Some of the controversy about Darwinian biology may have a related origin. Mother Nature, after all, does her own experiments in genetics. When her experiments succeed, we call the results evolution.

If evolution proceeds by experiments in genetics, and genetics experiments cannot be done with individuals, evolution is, by definition, a phenomenon of populations rather than individuals. Moreover, if Natural Selection plays the role of arbiter in evolution, and evolution is a population phenomenon, then Natural Selection must also be a population phenomenon. We will argue here that it is meaningless to speak of Natural Selection acting upon an individual without simultaneously taking into account what that individual does within its population.

Typically, a new genetic variant is introduced into a population by first arising in a single individual's germ line—that line of cells destined to produce gametes—and then being transmitted to that individual's offspring. If the variant expresses itself in dominant fashion, Natural Selection can have an immediate look at its worthiness. However, even if the variant is dominant, and certainly if it is recessive, the scrutiny cannot be complete until the homozygous combination is also tested.

In a species in which brother-sister (sib) matings occur, the emergence of homozygotes requires at least three generations, beginning with the individual in which the variant arose. The second generation consists of that individual's offspring, who can at most be heterozygotes for the new variant. Matings among brothers and sisters, known as sib matings, can then produce grand-offspring who are homozygotes. Where sib matings do not occur, Natural Selection cannot get a look at homozygotes until the fourth generation.

Against this background, we can now ask what it means to say that selection acts at the level of individuals or, as proponents of selfish genes would have it, at the level of the gene itself (it is critical here to separate the idea of gene as unit of selection from the idea of level of selection). In addressing this question, we are once again brought face-to-face with the idea that genes exist in a continuum. Natural Selection can scrutinize an individual carrying a new variant for eons of time, all to no avail. The individual is frozen in genetic time. Genetic experiments are conducted across time where the metric of time is successive generations.

Consider the dodo. The infamous extinction of that flightless island-dwelling bird is well known. There was presumably a moment in the history of dodos when only one remained. Suppose, for the sake of argument, that this was the most robust dodo that had ever been; it was full of the finest dodo genes. But even as Natural Selection scrutinized that fine dodo, nothing could come of it. That dodo was dead in the water.

The ultimate problem for dodos, of course, was that the final dodo lacked a mate. With a mate, that dodo and its fine genes might have prevailed.[7] But the process stalled because there was no mate. This is exactly equal to saying that the process stalled because there was no group—a dodo and its mate constitute the simplest group of dodos. There is simply no such thing as a self-made dodo.

The point we are forced to acknowledge is that selection, if confined to an individual, is a meaningless act. The manifestation of Natural Selection is precisely the act of transmitting genes to a subsequent generation and, in a sexually reproducing species, that is a group activity. It is impossible for Natural Selection to act outside the group. Selection can only see an individual within its lineage. Any evolutionary innovation, no matter how wonderful, has to be wonderful within the group in order to represent the lineage. The group thus serves as a filter through which every innovation passes, simultaneously enabling and constraining the evolutionary process. So we reiterate here that biological systems exist and change in a continuum and the continuum requires a group. By attempting to think about selection acting on an individual, we inadvertently convert that individual into a discontinuity. In the context of life, discontinuity is synonymous with extinction.

In addition to controversy about the level at which selection monitors genetic change in a species of organism, there is controversy about the mechanism by which selection effects and maintains evolutionary change. We already know that genes

84

provide the vehicle—it is genes that change across time. We also know that three fundamental properties of genes allow them to do this. Those three properties, we remind ourselves, are that they encode information, they are mutable and they are transmissible. The property of transmissibility subsumes the property that genes serve as templates for their own replication.

Two of these properties we can treat as essentially constant over evolutionary time. In the first place, for as long as DNA has been the genetic material, and we know it has been for a very long time, the mutability of genes can be treated as a constant. This constancy is reflected today in the observation that the full diversity of organisms, from bacteria, fungi, trees, and fruit flies, to laboratory rats and primates, each a vignette or glimpse of the evolutionary continuum, have comparable rates of mutational change, are susceptible to the same mutagenic agents and, indeed, undergo mutation by the same mechanisms. By the same token, if we monitor the way that genes are replicated and partitioned into daughter cells, these, too, are very similar across the spectrum.[8]

In contrast, if we measure the information content of genes from different organisms, we find that they are widely dissimilar. We mentioned earlier that this dissimilarity has the gratifying property of reflecting classical phylogenetic schemes—humans and chimps have very similar genetic content, humans and horses have quite dissimilar content and humans and flies are barely related. It is reasonable to say that evolution, at least over the range of organisms from bacteria to mammals, is much more a function of change in the message than in the nature of the messenger. The corollary is that, across time, Natural Selection scrutinizes the information content of genes. Natural Selection performs this scrutiny by inquiring how well the information is serving the group in which it exists.

These introductory thoughts on the properties of the genetic material bring us face-to-face with another curious construction in *The Selfish Gene*. In a passage devoted to finding the practical unit of Natural Selection, we are told that a gene must have these properties: longevity, fecundity and copying fidelity. The dichotomy between <u>longevity-fecundity-fidelity</u> and the alternative litany used here, <u>informational-mutable-transmissible</u>, is no doubt an amateur psychologist's bonanza. Our focus will be more narrow. We are in the middle of a debate about what Natural Selection is looking at when it selects.

Without too much difficulty, we can reconcile the properties of fecundity and fidelity with the alternative representations of transmissibility and mutability. The choice of words and the emphasis may be different, but they both contain the twin ideas of generating offspring and allowing for variability in those offspring.

86

When we turn our attention to the remaining property in each litany—longevity of the gene versus information content of the gene—we arrive at an irreconcilable difference.[9]   We will now visit the argument that the selfish gene idea is rooted in a fundamental misreading of the basis of Natural Selection.

This is actually our second visit to this part of the selfish gene controversy. In the last chapter we noted that *The Selfish Gene* contains the reasonable assertion that the gene is the basic unit of Natural Selection. However, this is followed by an invalid redefinition of the gene. That redefinition, you will recall, discards the classical definition that a gene is a single unit of function in favor of a definition based upon an arbitrary assembly of functional units that tend to be inherited together. In other words, the gene is newly defined as an entity of transmission from one generation to the next instead of an entity of information. It is loosely defined by its physical size, not rigorously defined by its explicit content. This physical entity, which may contain hundreds of classically defined genes, is then asserted to be the unit of Natural Selection. This redefinition of the gene suffers from the considerable deficiency that it confuses cause with effect. The cause of selective advantage is information content, monitored one nucleotide at a time.

We can demonstrate the validity of the classical gene by, once again, asking what happens when we follow genes through the continuum in which they exist. We will do this with the help of two genes, designated a and b, that occupy nearby sites on the same chromosome. Inasmuch as they are very close to each other, they are part of the unit of transmission envisaged in the selfish gene model—that is, they are part of one gene according to those who claim genes are selfish.

Suppose the population harbors variants of each of these genes, a_1 and b_1, that are advantageous to individuals who become homozygous for them. When a_1 and b_1 first arose, the population carried chromosomes that were almost all ab, with rare copies of a_1b and ab_1 (since variants arise infrequently, the probability that a_1 and b_1 would arise on the same copy of the chromosome is negligible). Since our discussion is about a diploid, sexually reproducing organism, the individuals in the population will be mostly ab/ab plus the two types of rare individuals that carry the new variants, ab/a_1b and ab/ab_1 (it might be worthwhile to draw simple diagrams of the seemingly repetitious exercise we will develop here). With time, additional pairwise combinations will be generated, including a_1b/a_1b and ab_1/ab_1. Since the homozygosity of a_1 and b_1 is advantageous, these chromosomes will increase in frequency. The increases in frequency of the homozygous individuals will cause an increase in frequency of individuals who are double heterozygotes, a_1b/ab_1. In such individuals, a recombination event between the sites of a_1 and b_1 will generate a chromosome that is a_1b_1 (see Appendix 2, inset b). As this chromosome spreads through the population, it will eventually be transmitted into single individuals by both parents. That is, double homozygotes, a_1b_1/a_1b_1, will be generated. Given that a_1/a_1 and b_1/b_1 are advantageous, a_1b_1/a_1b_1 individuals will have incremental advantage. *This can only be true if the unit of Natural Selection is a gene defined by function rather than transmission.*[10]

The delays between the times of appearance of a_1 and b_1 in the population, the subsequent generation of the a_1b_1 chromosomes and, subsequent to that, the appearance of a_1b_1/a_1b_1 homozygotes point up, once again, the importance of following genes through time. Since Mother Nature is very patient, attempting to understand her requires patience of us as well. Incidentally, the delay caused by the requirement to construct the a_1b_1 chromosome by recombination has the technical name linkage disequilibrium.

To this point, we have been dividing our attention between some thoughts about what genes are not:, genes are not selfish, and what genes are: genes are information. It is now time to examine the nature of genetic information more thoroughly and we turn to this task in the next chapter, some of which may require a little more effort of those with no background in biology. However, this will be expended in the pursuit of a deeper question that may justify such efforts: is there anything about genes that transcends simple information? We will ultimately derive the model that genes represent a search for truth.

As we prepare to leave *The Selfish Gene* (it will make another cameo appearance or two) we should acknowledge a caution it recommends. In an endnote to the New Edition (1989), the point is made (page 278) that a scholar with training in one field should be cautious when treading into another. In some of what follows, I will wander off into the subject of animal behavior. Since I am a layman in the area, the advice is well taken.

Finally, a general note on *The Selfish Gene*. If I were granted the privilege of editing the next edition, it would contain one wholesale change. Everywhere it uses the word *selfish*, the edited edition would contain the word *successful*. On the other hand, although the book would be vastly improved, *successful* still fails to capture what it is that genes really are.

6. A Little Theory of Everything

That which is not forbidden is mandatory.
  –an axiom of high energy physics

Much is forbidden; the rest is possible.
  –an axiom of Darwinian evolution

It is an axiom of the conventional wisdom that appearances can be deceiving. Nonetheless, in spite of the caution this might urge upon us, we oftentimes use appearances as the basis for judgments or decisions. In some cases we are being careless or following habit, while in other cases we may have little else to go on.

Our view of evolution is one of the things strongly influenced by appearances, especially by the succession of landmark events that so dominate the fossil record. Since the fossils reveal dramatic patterns of mass extinctions and expansions, it is tempting to see evolution itself in terms of these dramatic patterns. Darwin, however, imagined evolution to be a more or less gradual and constant process. I'm guessing he was right.

We noted earlier that fossils of simple cells are found in deposits known to be about three and one-half billion years old. Single-celled organisms have an exclusive hold on the fossil record until about 700 million years ago. The earliest known fossils of single eukaryotic cells are a little more than a billion years old. Beginning 700 million years ago and continuing for about 200 million years, there occurred a series of experiments in multicellular life. All modern fauna emerged from the organisms that first appeared during that period of time.

The 700-million-year-old Ediacaron Hills fauna (named after the site in Australia where first discovered) is apparently extinct. So, too, is the Tommotian fauna (similarly named after a site in Russia and about as old as the Ediacaron fauna). On the other hand, the Burgess fauna (named after the Burgess Shale in British Columbia) is about 500 million years old and contains representatives of all existing animal phyla, from sponges (sort of quasi-animals) to chordates like ourselves. A similar deposit to that at Burgess has recently been discovered in China. A brief description of the China site, in *National Geographic* (October, 1993), contains exquisite photographs of some of the fossils.

The geologically sudden appearance of all known animal groups, and an additional group of organisms which apparently have left no modern descendants, is so dramatic it has been given a name to reflect that drama—the Cambrian explosion. Animal life appears to have exploded onto the scene.

If the sudden appearance of multicellular life was dramatic, its aftermath can only be called astonishing. In the approximately five hundred million years since the Cambrian explosion, there have appeared dinosaurs, humming birds, honeybees, polar bears, jumping spiders, baleen whales and *Homo sapiens* (actually *Homo sapiens sapiens—Human wise wise or Human smart smart*; one supposes the name to have been thought up by a human). These biological entities, the ones at which we tend to marvel, occupy little more than the most recent ten percent of evolutionary time.

At first glance, it seems paradoxical that the unicellular phase of evolution was such a painfully slow process. In contrast, multicellular life not only burst onto the scene, but has also been characterized by great paroxysms of evolutionary expansions and even more calamitous extinctions. This appearance of saltatory behavior in the fossil record of multicellular organisms has caused widespread interest in a neo-Darwinian view that evolution itself is erratic, proceeding apace in some periods but remaining more or less static in others. According to this school of thought, the classical Darwinian notion of a steady accumulation of favorable traits *via* Natural Selection must be replaced by the modern notion of stasis alternating with instability and change. This model has been given the name punctuated equilibrium. I am going to develop here the argument that saltations or punctuations of equilibria are actually predicted by classical Darwinism. This argument is nowhere more tenable than at the Cambrian explosion itself.

The approach we will follow in this argument will be the devil's advocacy that the pre-Cambrian phase of life—the inventing and refining of single cells—was in fact more sensational than the subsequent appearance of the most horrible lizard. That is, inventing the single cell was more impressive than inventing *Tyrannosaurus rex*, using, as the starting point for accomplishing the latter feat, the single cells that were already on hand. We will explore this proposition through the simple expedient of reviewing certain properties of single cells. After that review, we will ask what additional properties of single cells would equip them for multicellular life and how such properties might have been acquired. We will then essay the perhaps surprising conclusion that the Cambrian explosion may look like an explosion at the level of organisms but doesn't look at all like an explosion at the level of cells. Cells, and therefore the genes inside cells, did not need to change much at the transition from unicellular to multicellular existence. After all, by definition, all of the innovations required to begin a multicellular existence had to occur in unicellular organisms. The alternative view, that organisms became multicellular first and then acquired the innovations of multicellular existence, would present us with severe logical difficulties.

At this point in our text we will also rejoin the theme that genes are information and begin to explore the nature of genetic information. We have already touched on the technical side of this question—the concern with what genes are made of, and how that substance facilitates the storage and expression of information.

Another side to the question deals more with the quality of genetic information in the sense of its value. Perhaps we can see this most clearly by putting ourselves in Mother Nature's shoes. What, in fact, does Mother Nature value in a gene? What does Natural Selection select when it looks at a gene? When we ask these questions, we come to see a single operational criterion that runs through every facet of evolution—from the very beginning of life to the advent of mammalian nervous systems. Natural Selection always asks this of a genetic change: do you cause some improvement in recognition of your immediate environment? Since life is part of the immediate environment, repeatedly asking this question will lead to life's recognition of itself.

A proper review of the functions of a single cell would fill several thousand pages. Since we do not have that luxury, we can only describe a small number of cellular features and extrapolate their effects. This approach would work best if there were a set of core principles we could expound and generalize. Happily, such core principles exist, the most fundamental of which is something called the Central Dogma, and it embodies just the sort of starting point we need.

The Central Dogma consists of the litany that DNA (the material of genes) is transcribed into RNA (the messenger that allows stored information to become expressed information), which is translated into protein (the ultimate object of information storage and retrieval). As we proceed through a description of the workings of the Central Dogma, you will notice that we are dealing the technical aspect of genetic information in anticipation of dealing with what we described above as the value of genetic information.

BIOSYNTHESIS VIA TEMPLATE-BASED RECOGNITION

We will begin our review of the Central Dogma by outlining the synthesis of a protein, one of the most complex activities in Mother Nature's repertory. It is therefore useful to bear in mind that the underlying principles are few and straightforward. In the first place, protein synthesis is literally a translation from one language to another. Information stored in the nucleic acid language, written in nucleotide words, is translated into the protein language, written in amino acid words. Both of these languages use linear arrays of words and punctuations. Secondly, every step in the process utilizes the chemical property of molecular recognition. The collection of recognitions that constitute protein synthesis is a very special collection, to be sure.

The list below is a subset of the molecular components required within a cell for protein synthesis to occur. Over the course of our discussion, we will indicate what these various components are,

96

how they arise and how their activities and properties contribute to cellular function.

1. The first component on our list is a protein molecule called **RNA polymerase** (which is actually a complex of molecules).
2. The second component is a segment of a chromosome containing **one gene**.
3. We add to this another complex and, in molecular terms, gigantic structure called a **ribosome**.
4. The fourth component is a pool of specialized RNA molecules called **transfer RNAs**.
5. The fifth, and for now last, component is a pool of **precursors**. These include **nucleotide triphosphates**, the subunits used in the production of RNA (Appendix 1), and **amino acids**, the subunits used in the production of proteins (Appendix 3).

The components above are major players in the mechanism by which *stored* genetic information, in the form of a gene, becomes *expressed* genetic information, in the form of a protein. We now outline the process by which DNA information becomes protein information, leaving out some details and rearranging others, but not in a way that will affect the final form or validity of the outline (a schematic representation of this process is given in Appendix 4).

Two of the components in the list above are found in the nucleus if the organism we are observing is eukaryotic.[2] One of these components, the RNA polymerase complex, recognizes and binds to a specific part of the second component, the gene itself. This binding takes place at one end of the gene, where there occurs a specific sequence of nucleotide base pairs. The direct meaning of this sequence to RNA polymerase can be stated as follows: this is a site on the chromosome that you recognize and you enact that recognition by binding to this site. The indirect meaning of this sequence—what emerges as the interpretation of this site—can be stated as follows: a gene starts here.

The technical name for a site that means "a gene starts here" is promoter. Promoters were first discovered in bacteria. The studies that led to this discovery were done at the Pasteur Institute in Paris in the early 1960's by a group of scientists who had decided to tackle fundamental questions about biology through the study of bacteria and the viruses that infect them. We pointed out earlier that the use of model systems came to characterize the emergence of molecular biology. The phenomenon was international.

Meanwhile, in the cell we have under scrutiny, a molecule of RNA polymerase has recognized a promoter, and betrays this act of recognition by binding to the promoter. It interprets this site as the start of a gene and begins a lateral migration along the chromosome towards that gene. At the same time, it begins to catalyze the synthesis of an RNA molecule that is a copy of the gene (Appendix 4; the meaning of catalysis falls roughly between causing the synthesis and enabling the synthesis). The RNA molecule produced in this synthesis is complementary to the strand from which it is copied and identical in sequence to the other, uncopied strand of the DNA. There is the caveat that RNA is synthesized with the pyrimidine base uracil (U) in place of the base thymine that occurs in DNA (Appendix 1). For example, if RNA polymerase were copying the DNA sequence:

ATGC
TACG

in a left to right direction from the bottom strand, the resulting RNA product would be **AUGC** (i.e., **AUGC** of RNA is complementary to **TACG** of DNA or, equally valid, the DNA sequence **TACG** served as the template for the synthesis of the **AUGC** copy). Thus, the relationship of an RNA molecule to DNA is like that of the two DNA strands to each other—it is complementary to the strand from which it is copied and identical to the other strand (remembering the **U** for **T** substitution).

If an RNA molecule is copied from a length of DNA that is 900 base pairs long, the RNA molecule will thus be 900 bases long (the synthesis of an RNA molecule stops at a sequence of nucleotides in the

DNA that convey the message "this gene ends here" and the polymerase disengages). The resulting RNA molecule will be transported to the part of the cell outside the nucleus (the cytoplasm) and its nucleic acid message translated into protein language.

The role of RNA polymerase in this process can be thought of as two-fold. First, it facilitates the alignment of the RNA subunits with the complementary bases of the DNA sequence it is copying. Secondly, it catalyzes the formation of the chemical bonds that link the subunits into the growing RNA chain (These chemical bonds in RNA are identical to the linkages of phosphates to sugars you see in each of the two backbones of the DNA molecule illustrated in Appendix 1). Subunits are added at a rate of about fifty per second with about one error in ten thousand additions. This sort of speed and fidelity is typical of biological processes.

Armed with this brief description of what happens in the synthesis of a molecule of messenger RNA (abbreviated mRNA) we can now ask a slightly more difficult question—how does this happen? We already introduced the idea that RNA polymerase recognizes the part of a gene called its promoter and binds there. Either component of the system is unreactive with other materials but reacts avidly with its counterpart. A crude analogy is the binding of Velcro® strips.

The next step in polymerase activity involves more complex levels of recognition. The RNA polymerase-promoter complex is joined by the first nucleotide subunit which is recognized by the polymerase as a proper subunit (i.e., it is a purine or pyrimidine base) and, *via* the interaction of the subunit with DNA, as *the* proper subunit. If, for example, the first base to be copied in DNA is T, the subunit selected for RNA synthesis will be A. The polymerase molecule now moves along the gene to the next base. If the second base is A, polymerase facilitates the selection of U, based on the mutual recognition of U and A.

This second act of recognition causes the first selected subunit, A, to be juxtaposed to the second selected subunit, U. This configuration is recognized by the catalytic site on the polymerase molecule which then catalyzes the formation of the chemical bond (in the sugar-phosphate backbone) that holds A and U together as the first two members of the growing chain (when the subunits have been thus connected they are oftentimes referred to as residues of the RNA molecule).

The process described here continues sequentially down the DNA molecule until reaching the termination sequence, mentioned above, that means "the gene ends here." This termination sequence is recognized by the synthetic system as the message to un-bind from the DNA. In other words, every step in the synthesis of RNA, from the initial binding of polymerase to the promoter, to the un-binding from the termination sequence, is a specific event of recognition (although termination can be thought of as a specific failure of recognition).

The just-synthesized RNA message, a polymer consisting of hundreds of subunits, is now ready for transport out of the nucleus to the cytoplasm. We will not dwell on the mechanism of this transport (or specific acts of editing carried out on the newly synthesized RNA molecule), but should note in passing that it is not passive and, like the other steps in this process, involves specific acts of recognition.

Once in the cytoplasm, the mRNA meets up with two other of our starting components, a ribosome and a particular species of transfer RNA (tRNA) which we will describe below. The mRNA, tRNA and ribosome bind to each other, again through acts of specific recognition. The binding of mRNA to tRNA and ribosome always occurs near the end of the mRNA that was first synthesized.

The precise point on the mRNA at which it binds to the tRNA is special—the first occurrence of the triplet sequence AUG. This triplet of nucleotides is recognized by the complementary sequence in tRNA, UAC (Appendixes 3 and 4). The UAC sequence in the tRNA is known as the anticodon to the AUG codon. We should also note that the tRNA itself is a gene product. Thus, somewhere in the chromosomes of the cell we are watching, there is a sequence of nucleotides, in DNA double helical form, that is transcribed by RNA polymerase to yield the single-stranded tRNA.

102

It will by now come as no surprise that the site on the ribosome at which the mRNA-tRNA-ribosome association occurs is also special. It is called the P-site (Peptidyl-tRNA site). In sum, we have a specific codon (at a specific place in the message), a specific anticodon (at a specific place in the tRNA) and a specific site in the ribosome engaging together in a compound act of recognition (see Appendix 4 to visualize this arrangement).

A second property of the tRNA molecule with the UAC anticodon is that it always has attached to it the amino acid methionine—we can call it tRNA-methionine or tRNA$_{met}$ (Appendixes 3 and 4). This attachment is achieved through the action of an enzyme that simultaneously recognizes and binds to methione and to the tRNA, catalyzes their union and dissociates from them, ready to perform this feat again for other copies of the same tRNA and amino acid. This relationship, the existence of a specific tRNA and a specific enzyme that always attaches the same amino acid to that tRNA, is true for all tRNAs and amino acids. That is, a given type of tRNA always carries the same amino acid. Furthermore, that tRNA always has a particular anticodon and thus recognizes the same codon in a molecule of mRNA. We will see below how this set of properties allows a given message to be translated into a specific protein.

The enzyme that catalyzes the attachment of a particular amino acid to a particular tRNA is called an amino-acyl-tRNA-synthetase. Each such enzyme, one for each combination of amino acid and tRNA, is itself a gene product and thus produced by the same process of protein synthesis we are in the middle of describing.

We have already assembled a complex of ribosome, mRNA and tRNA$_{met}$. The tRNA is sitting in the P-site of the ribosome and its anticodon (UAC) is joined to the first AUG codon in the mRNA. This complex is now ready to begin synthesizing the protein molecule encoded by this particular messenger RNA. The next step in the process is the recognition of the adjacent triplet codon in the mRNA molecule by the appropriate tRNA. Suppose the adjacent codon is UUU. It will be recognized by the anticodon AAA. The tRNA bearing this anticodon always has attached to it the amino acid phenylalanine, placed there through the action of an amino-acyl-tRNA-synthetase that recognizes both phenlyalanine and the tRNA with the anticodon AAA. This tRNA we can thus abbreviate as tRNA$_{phe}$.

The act of associating with the UUU codon brings the tRNA$_{phe}$ into a position on the ribosome called the A-site (Amino-acyl tRNA site). The A-site is immediately adjacent to the P-site. Since the AUG codon sitting in the P-site is adjacent to the UUU codon sitting in the A-site, the tRNAs associated with them are caused to be adjacent to each other. Furthermore, the amino acids methionine and phenylalanine, attached to these adjacent tRNAs, are thus brought into juxtaposition. Precisely at the point of the association of the two amino acids with each other and with the ribosome, there sits on the ribosome an enzymatic activity called peptidyl transferase. Peptidyl transferase catalyzes the joining of methionine to phenylalanine to form what is called a di-peptide, and protein synthesis is under way (*peptide* is a synonym for *protein*). The bond formed by this enzymatic action is called a peptide bond and is the fundamental bond linking the series of amino acid subunits together that form a protein (Appendix 3). If you have no prior experience with the mechanism of protein synthesis, this might be a good time to gaze for a while at the diagrammatic representation in Appendix 4.

The next step in protein synthesis is no less amazing. The methionine attachment to $tRNA_{met}$ is broken by the formation of the peptide bond with phenylalanine; $tRNA_{met}$ leaves the P-site and $tRNA_{phe}$ and the UUU codon with which it is still associated ratchet into the P-site from the A-site. Notice also that $tRNA_{phe}$ still has attached to it the amino acid phenylalanine, which, in turn, has the amino acid methionine attached to it (this is the nascent protein). The A-site is now vacant except for the next triplet codon in the message. Suppose the next codon is AAG. It will be recognized by the anticodon UUC, which is contained in a tRNA to which the amino acid lysine is always attached (by the appropriate amino-acyl-tRNA-synthetase). A peptide bond is now formed between phenylalanine and lysine, tRNA$_{phe}$ is released from the P-site and tRNA$_{lys}$ ratchets into the P-site. This process continues until the end of the protein is reached—one hundred amino acids subunits is a relatively small protein while a protein of fifteen hundred amino acids is relatively large. The rate of addition of amino acids to a growing polypeptide—i.e., the rate of ratcheting through the P- and A-sites—can be as much as forty cycles per second. Depending upon the cell type and the protein being synthesized, it may also be occurring simultaneously on as many as forty or fifty thousand ribosomes. Cells can produce lots of protein in short order.

The cessation of protein synthesis is achieved by an explicit termination step. This step is made possible by the fact that no tRNA species carry anticodons to the triplets UAA, UAG and UGA. When one of these triplets enters the A-site, synthesis is stopped by the intervention of a termination factor which causes the ribosome-mRNA-protein complex to disassemble. The mRNA and the ribosome are free to re-associate (either with each other, or the mRNA with another ribosome and the ribosome with another message) and repeat the process.

The nature and properties of any protein synthesized in this system is a direct function of the sequence of amino acids in that protein. For example, one sequence of amino acids yields the protein hemoglobin ß. Another amino acid sequence yields the protein actin, a major component of muscle. Yet another sequence yields the enzyme amino-acyl-tRNA-synthetase-lysine, and so on. The sequences of amino acids in these and all other proteins are dictated by the sequence of ribonucleotides in the mRNAs from which they are translated.[11] The sequence of ribonuleotides in a messenger RNA is dictated, in turn, by the sequence of nucleotide base pairs in the gene from which that particular mRNA is transcribed.

With this overview of protein synthesis, we can now begin to get some sense of the magnitude of the economy of a single cell. Suppose we take as our starting point a cell that has just come into being as one of two cells generated by the division of a pre-existing or mother cell. We would like to call this a new cell, but there are ways in which this is not exactly so. For example, for this cell to begin expressing any of its genes, it must contain RNA polymerase. The RNA polymerase it contains at the outset was necessarily manufactured in the mother cell and packaged into the daughter or new cell. In fact, everything in this cell, at the moment of its birth, was manufactured in the mother cell. To a first approximation, it is a new cell comprised entirely of used components. We are reminded by this of the continuity of life.

A new cell has basically one of two possible fates. It might be a terminally differentiated cell such as a red blood cell or a neuron. Such a cell does not divide again and assumes its specific function depending upon which genes within the cell have been expressed during its development.[12]   For example, genes encoding hemoglobin are expressed during production of red blood cells; red blood cells are packed with hemoglobin and do not divide further. Genes encoding neuro-transmitters and other specific products are expressed during development of a neuron, and so on for each type of cell.

The second type of fate for a new cell is to remain more generalized and to divide to produce daughter cells of its own. Most cells of an early developing embryo fall into this category, and adults contain a variety of cells that divide throughout their lives. The latter cells, mostly of a class known as stem cells, continue to produce daughter cells that become, for example, red blood cells, or epithelial cells of tissue such as skin and so on (different kinds of stem cells produce different kinds of daughter cells).

A new cell whose fate it is to divide into two daughters must accomplish a number of specific prerequisites for division. One of these is to make two copies of all the genetic information it contains— i.e., duplicate its chromosomes. The process of duplicating chromosomes through synthesis of DNA bears a strong resemblance to the process of synthesizing RNA. The synthesis of DNA is carried out by an enzyme called DNA polymerase (like RNA polymerase, DNA polymerase is actually a complex aggregate of enzymatic functions). Numerous

108

molecules of DNA polymerase begin the process of duplicating chromosomes by recognizing a specific sequence of nucleotides and binding to the chromosomes at all sites containing that sequence. Each chromosome has many such sites, each of which is called an origin of replication or simply an origin. The recognition and binding of DNA polymerase to an origin is entirely analogous to the recognition and binding of RNA polymerase to a promoter. However, origins and promoters are distinct. RNA polymerase recognizes promoter sequences and DNA polymerase recognizes origin sequences.

The synthetic steps utilized to copy or replicate DNA are extraordinarily similar to those used for RNA synthesis. A growing DNA molecule is elongated one nucleotide at a time; each added nucleotide is chosen as the complement to the nucleotide in the strand being copied. That is, the same rules of recognition are employed in both DNA and RNA synthesis. There are, however, three fundamental distinctions between DNA and RNA synthesis. DNA polymerase recognizes and employs deoxyribonucleotides instead of ribonuleotides. Secondly, in the process of DNA replication, both strands are copied simultaneously (as opposed to just one of the two strands in RNA synthesis). Thirdly, the newly synthesized strand does not separate from its template. Instead, it permanently replaces the original complementary strand (permanently that is, until the next time the chromosome is replicated).

Since this occurs simultaneously to both strands of the original double helix, the end result is two complete double helices. In other words, there emerge two copies of each chromosome in the cell nucleus. With respect to chromosomes, the cell is now ready to divide. However, there are many other things that must first be accomplished.

Indeed, replicating the chromosomes is one of the last things the new cell does in preparation for division. Imagine that the cell we are following is a human cell. Prior to replication, the chromosomes in that cell contain about twelve billion nucleotide subunits. The feat of replicating those chromosomes, therefore, requires a pool of free subunits containing at least three billion of each type (assuming that the number of A:T base pairs is equal to the number of G:C base pairs, which is roughly true for human DNA). Those subunits must be either imported or synthesized—we will deal here with the simpler case of intracellular synthesis.

BIOSYNTHESIS VIA SUBSTRATE RECOGNITION

Synthesis of a molecule like a pyrimidine (or a purine or amino acid) occurs through biosynthetic pathways that, in stepwise fashion, build these complex organic molecules by combining simpler organic and inorganic precursors. Part of the biosynthetic pathway for pyrimidines is shown in Appendix 5 as an example.

110

Each step in this biosynthesis is catalyzed by an enzyme with high specificity for the biochemical reaction occurring in that step. The enzyme recognizes the substrates of the reaction, brings them into close proximity to each other, and catalyzes their union to form the product(s) of the reaction. Since the reaction occurs in the absence of a template, the product of the reaction isn't a copy of an existing molecule or template, but is more akin to something invented or created by the enzyme. The enzyme, of course, is a gene-encoded protein so that the apparent inventiveness of the enzyme actually reflects a genetic discovery at the level of nucleic acids, chanced upon in the first place, and fixed by Natural Selection.

It is not always easy to grasp the power and efficacy of the biological recognitions encoded in genes. As a case in point, consider a cell preparing to replicate its DNA—a process that takes less than a day. In that period of time, such a cell must produce several billion nucleotides. (In a human cell, with twelve billion nucleotides in its chromosomes, the pyrimidine pathway illustrated in Appendix 5 has to perform each step six billion times. An equally elaborate pathway of purine biosynthesis must do the same.) Meanwhile, the cell has other and greater problems of economy. For example, it must manufacture very large numbers of proteins. Leaving aside for the moment the various enzymes we have mentioned, we can focus on other types of proteins produced in especially great quantities, for example, those with structural and kinetic functions.

One very abundant family of proteins is that known as the histones. These proteins recognize and bind to DNA. Unlike the polymerase molecules, however, histones bind to DNA in a regular and repeating fashion, without much regard for special nucleotide sequences such as promoters and origins. As a consequence of their binding to DNA, histones play a critical role in stabilizing DNA and in the folding of chromosomes in preparation for cell division (chromosomes are condensed or shortened about ten thousand-fold during cell division, facilitating their separation into daughter cells). As the cell prepares to divide, it must double the number of histone molecules since it has doubled its chromosomes, also in preparation for division. Cells such as our own contain about 300 million of these proteins.

As proteins go, the histones are rather small, ranging from about 100 to 200 amino acids in length. Using the lower figure of 100 amino acids per protein molecule, so that we error on the side of caution, we estimate that the cell must synthesize or import thirty billion amino acid subunits [(100 amino acids per protein molecule) X (300 million protein molecules)], each time it prepares to divide. The synthesis of these thirty billion subunits is a fine beginning, but let us not forget the need for their subsequent polymerization into proteins, translated on ribosomes from the appropriate mRNA molecules. In the same twenty-four hour period allotted for the production of subunits, protein synthesis must be initiated 300 million times, and twenty nine billion, seven hundred million peptide bonds must be formed (three hundred million proteins with ninety-nine bonds per protein). Attempting to visualize the logistics involved is a worthy (and worthwhile) challenge.

In addition to the large synthetic requirements for the duplication of chromosomes, there is another great need for material to duplicate the cell's packaging system. Each cell is separated from its external environment by a bilayer membrane and also has an extensive internal membrane system. One example of the latter is the nuclear membrane which, except during cell division, separates the chromosomes from the rest of the cell interior. Appendix 6 shows the structure of one of the major components of membranes—a phospholipid—and a schematic of the way these molecules interact to form the bilayer.[13]

The number of phospholipid molecules in an average eukaryotic cell is on the order of two billion. Thus, making two cells where there was one requires the manufacture of two billion of these membrane building blocks. The pathway by which these molecules are manufactured has a complexity comparable to that of the pyrimidine pathway employed in earlier illustrations. As with the pyrimidine pathway, each step in the pathway

113

producing phospholipids must function billions of times before a cell can complete a division cycle.

While the examples cited above are probably sufficient to make the point that a cell has daunting metabolic requirements, we must not fail to consider the need for energy. The primary energy currency in a cell is the same adenosine triphosphate, or ATP, that we have already seen as a major component of RNA and, in its deoxyribose form, of DNA.

The full story of ATP generation and utilization requires an ample textbook. It begins in photosynthesis, where energy from sunlight is captured and utilized to synthesize sugars.[14] The energy, initially stored in the chemical bonds of sugar molecules, becomes transferred to the bonds that connect phosphate groups to adenosine molecules (the generation of ATP is outlined in Appendix 7). The energy stored in phosphate bonds of ATP, unlike the energy stored in the bonds in sugar molecules, can be used directly in the large majority of energy-requiring functions within a cell. For example, generating a peptide bond in protein synthesis requires ATP.[15] The muscle contractions that allow you to walk from here to there also require ATP.

For the sake of streamlining the argument, suppose that the synthesis of every cellular building block requires the expenditure of one molecule of ATP (this is a vast underestimate). In this accounting scheme, the cost of every amino acid, every nucleotide and every phospholipid is one ATP. Suppose further that every bond formed in the synthesis of proteins, RNA and DNA also exacts this price. Since billions of building blocks and bonds are required for one cell to duplicate all of its structures, multiple billions of ATP molecules are also required. Indeed, for present purposes, we can comfortably settle on an estimate of a trillion ATP molecules per cell per generation. For reference, a trillion ATP molecules can be generated by tapping the usable energy contained in about 300 billion molecules of the sugar glucose. The mass or weight of this much glucose is about a billionth of a gram. While that surely strikes us as extraordinary, we should note well that the story of large numbers on a small scale is as old as the cosmos.

In a dividing cell, as in the cosmos, the outcome of the interactions of large numbers of building blocks and energy units depends also upon the timing of events. A more or less typical eukaryotic cell, such as one of our own, duplicates itself in a day or so. That is, in the course of a single day, a cell can manufacture or assimilate billions of complex molecular building blocks and utilize a trillion molecules of ATP. The end-products are two cells, virtually identical to the single cell from which they are derived. Mother Nature has built an incredibly accurate and efficient machine.

Beyond accuracy and efficiency, there are other striking features of this handiwork. One of these is parsimony. We have already seen the example of ATP, which does multiple duty as the cell's major energy carrier, an essential building block of RNA and, in its deoxyribose form, an essential building block of DNA (see Appendixes 1 and 7). The use of one entity for multiple applications is seen repeatedly at every level of biological organization.

The idea of parsimony applies to re-use as surely as it does to multiple use. Mother Nature is a fanatical recycler. The trillion or so molecules of ATP, used by a single cell in the process of becoming two, is actually more on the order of a billion molecules, each of which is re-used a thousand times. A simplified scheme for the process of recycling ATP is included in Appendix 7.

The brief overview that we have developed here for the economy of a single cell is really a part of the iceberg. In addition to histones, for example, there are other kinds of protein molecules present in massive quantities. Among these, the proteins of the cytoskeleton confer upon cells the capacity to assume shapes other than spherical, to have elasticity and the capacity for certain types of cellular movement.

Most proteins within a cell are present in more modest numbers. Enzymes are typically represented by hundreds or thousands of copies. Similarly, there are proteins inserted across the plasma membrane—transmembrane proteins—that are also present in smaller numbers. On the other hand, there are thousands of such proteins. Taken as a group, they

116

represent another large investment in precursor molecules and in the energy for their synthesis.

The fact that the cell must produce many types of products, some in very large quantities, introduces the potential for a logistics nightmare. However, Mother Nature is a very skilled manager and no logistical problems occur. Not only are parts manufactured in appropriate numbers to appropriate specifications, but they are also manufactured in the right place at the right time. The world's most talented engineers can only stand aside and marvel at the organization, complexity and efficiency of the single cell. In the space of a day, it can turn out trillions of products of tens of thousands of designs and functions, with consummate placement and timing. And the processes by which these things are accomplished are almost error-free.

We should be hesitant to push the engineering metaphor too far—it could seem to trivialize living systems. Nonetheless, if we think of metabolic systems as engineering on a cosmic scale, and inquire what sorts of principles are involved, some useful generalizations emerge.

From the engineering perspective, we first see that Mother Nature invests heavily in Research and Development. Natural Selection might be likened to accepting certain products (or prototypes) for further refinement and testing. These products are also finished to very close tolerances. Every biological product has extremely highly refined recognition of its place and time in the cellular economy. The concept of place includes recognition of the task, and of the site where that task is performed. Since the system builds itself, quality control is intrinsic.

Living systems also have highly selective and sensitive feedback loops. For example, subunit inventories are managed through participation of the subunits themselves. A high level of a particular subunit, such as a nucleotide base or an amino acid, can act directly, by negative feedback, to shut down the assembly line by which it is produced.

All of the biological properties we have considered to this point depend upon two features of subunits and their polymers. The first feature is molecular recognition. We have seen that nucleotides recognize their complements and that enzymes recognize their substrates, for example. Secondly, behaviors flow from these recognitions. DNA and RNA can be synthesized from templates because of nucleotide complementarity and specific enzymatic reactions. Proteins can be synthesized from heterologous templates because of mRNA-tRNA (codon-anticodon) complementarity followed by specific enzymatic reactions. Each of the remarkable feats performed by the single cell is made possible by one or more precise and avid acts of recognition.

People of certain temperaments and training are inclined to look upon the remarkable properties of a single cell with its astonishing capacity to become

118

two cells and see some form of magic at work. They might argue, for example, that these fundamental biological activities have too much order to represent the product of anything so apparently haphazard as Darwinian evolution.

Other people, of differing temperament and persuasion, look upon these same properties and events and conclude that this simply could not have arisen by an act of magic. It must have arisen, instead, by the accretion of order through iterative acts of Natural Selection. Although favorable genetic variants are known indeed to arise initially by chance, once selected into the framework of living systems, they are no longer chance. They become the order and necessity upon which the subsequent iterations of variation and selection can build. As always, we emphasize that these iterations have been unfolding on a time scale measured in billions of years.

Earlier in this chapter, we addressed the apparent paradox that life existed only as single cells for the first three billion years of evolutionary time, whereas it took a tenth that length of time—something on the order of 300 million years—to progress from the first experiments in multicellular life to the invention of the dinosaurs. That is, Mother Nature has spent ten times longer in the development of the single cell than in elaboration of this single cell into large and complex animals. While we can all agree, no doubt, that enormous reptiles are notable achievements, we are forced to harbor a grave suspicion that the invention of the single cell is the more spectacular achievement.

We can gain a fuller appreciation for the feat of inventing the single cell by having a second look at the workings of a biosynthetic pathway from a slightly different perspective. We earlier introduced the pathway for pyrimidine synthesis as an example of the synthetic facet of cellular activity. We would like to know how such pathways might have been designed and built, given that life had to invent them from scratch. One biologist (Horowitz, 1961) has devised a model which, as they say in the trade, is too pretty not to be true.

Horowitz' model begins at the point which is common to all thinking on the origin of life from its pre-biotic beginnings. There are powerful reasons, on astronomical grounds, for thinking that the pre-biotic atmosphere of the earth contained various gases, such as nitrogen (N_2), carbon dioxide (CO_2), methane (CH_4) and water (H_2O). That early atmosphere would also have been subjected to physical forces, such as ultraviolet radiation and electrical discharge in the form of lightning.

If a mixture of gases like that above is introduced into a laboratory vessel and subjected to electrical discharge, there results the production of complex organic molecules, including amino acids. Variations on this experimental theme have produced nucleotides and sugars (Miller and Orgel, 1974). In

120

other words, the fundamental building blocks of life are surprisingly easy to manufacture by non-biological processes. We should note that some or all of the initial building blocks for life could also have had a non-terrestrial origin. There is increasing evidence that molecules like nucleotides and amino acids exist in non-terrestrial space and arrive on earth in substantial quantities as parts of vehicles like meteorites.

Given the existence of building blocks, the first natural experiments tending in the direction of life were surely spontaneous assembly of nucleotides, or nucleotide-like molecules, into autocatalytic, self replicating polymers. One of the consequences of this experimentation with self-replicating polymers would have been that the subunits used to manufacture them would eventually become incorporated into polymers and thus depleted—even in the vast, shallow seas that covered the early earth. The experiment in self replication would have ceased at that point unless one of the proto-organisms discovered a way to manufacture subunits from previously untapped resources.

Human experimentation with evolving molecular systems in laboratory settings is still in its infancy, but enough has been learned in the last decade to suggest a rationale for the natural experiments. All indications are that the prototype nucleic acid polymers were RNA. Not only can RNA molecules be translated into peptide sequences, but there is a growing literature on catalytic (enzymatic) and autocatalytic (self-assembly) functions of RNA. (e.g., Cech, 1986). A popular account of some current research into self-replication can be found in Rebek, 1994.

Given the intrinsic reactivity of RNA molecules, there was probably little delay between their advent, the first forays into the world of template behavior, and experimentation with peptide biosynthesis. Moreover, the early translations did not need be very elaborate to have striking consequences. Recent studies have shown that very small peptides—five to six amino acids in length—possess surprising biological activity (Houghton, 1993). When we couple the recent insights into RNA function to the obvious advantage accruing to a proto-organism with minimal biosynthetic capabilities, the invention of biosynthetic systems begins to appear much more straightforward than we had previously thought.

For illustration, picture an RNA-based proto-organism making copies of itself and spreading through the ancient seas. One of the things we can know about this entity is that it would become increasingly variable—the process of like begetting approximately like would have been there at the beginning, in the same way that it is unavoidable today. Secondly, it, or more accurately they, would gradually deplete the supply of pyrimidines (and purines) they had been using to make those copies. However, there are related pyrimidines they had not been using, among them orotic acid (refer again to Appendix 5). The first of these self-replicating molecules to possess catalytic activity towards amino acids, and to generate a little peptide with even the most modest enzyme-like ability to convert orotic acid to uracil, would have averted a sort of molecular starvation. Stated more positively, it would have created the circumstances to allow the experiment in replication to proceed by tapping a new source of subunits.

The newly discovered conversion of orotic acid to uracil could be very inefficient and the ancient enzyme could function very crudely—any unique exploitation of previously untapped resources would bestow a sensational advantage on the proto-organism that possessed this capability. Time is not of the essence. A million years or ten million years are of no great moment. There are no predators and, although the proto-organism cannot know it, billions of years lay before it.

A modified proto-organism with the capacity to exploit orotic acid in its environment would eventually encounter the same problem its ancestor did: its resource base would become depleted. In the view of Horowitz, the solution to this problem follows the same rationale as the solution to the initial resource problem. In the present case, a crude enzymatic activity that converts dihydroorotate to orotic acid (Appendix 5), occurring in a representative of the proto-organism that has already become an orotic acid utilizer, once again bestows advantage on this emerging line of genetic descent.

Continued application of this logic creates an evolutionary ratchet, leading back to the first step of pyrimidine biosynthesis. The end result is the invention of a pathway that constructs complex molecules from very simple molecules, easily obtained from the environment. We enter here the caveat that some of the steps in the pathway make use of more complex molecules like amino acids. However, amino acids are among the most common organic molecules to be synthesized by non-biological means, and would have been readily available for this utilization. Moreover, utilizing amino acids would establish a powerful selective advantage for the first crude discoveries leading to their synthesis—by the same rationale we've outlined here for nucleotides.

The inventions of biosynthetic pathways are landmark events. Pondering these inventions contributes to our understanding of the vast stretches of time that elapsed in the perfection of the single cell. It also generates some compelling predictions. For example, given the key role of nucleotides in the emergence of self-replicating proto-organisms, we would expect that their biosynthetic pathways would be among the most ancient. It is noteworthy, therefore, that the sequence of steps in the synthesis of pyrimdines is exactly identical in cells ranging from the bacteria to eukaryotes like ourselves. Similarly, the biosynthesis of purines is the same in all organisms. The metabolism of glucose, the central fixture of energy utilization in the vast majority of cells on earth, and a process that unfolds over about twenty biochemical steps, is virtually identical in all cells, from bacteria to mammals. It would appear that the pathways most near the core of life evolved in the earliest stages of life, and have been retained by all the descendants of our first ancestors. None of these central wheels has been re-invented.

A second set of predictions from the Horowitz model concerns the relationship of adjacent steps in an emerging biosynthetic pathway. For two reasons, we would expect the evolution of the second step in the pathway (counting in the backwards direction from the end-product of the pathway) to occur more easily than the first step. In the first place, the invention of step one of the pathway also represents the invention of protein synthesis. Although the first peptides had to have been synthesized as genetic accidents, as soon as one of them proved beneficial to the proto-organism in which it had become encoded, that organism received feedback about the existence of that peptide. One might say that the first useful peptide informed the organism that the process it had tumbled to, peptide synthesis, was worth improving. The capacity for Darwinian descent through modification by Natural Selection had turned an important corner. From that point on, it became easier to invent a new protein because the machinery for protein synthesis was itself now in place and under the scrutiny of Natural Selection.

Another boon to the evolution of the second step of a biosynthetic pathway stems from the very existence of the first step. Still using the pyrimidine pathway for illustration, we can note the structural similarity of uracil, orotic acid and dihydro-orotic acid. Since these structures are very similar to each other, it is easy to imagine that the enzyme that recognizes orotic acid and converts it to uracil would have the potential, with just a little modification, to become an enzyme that recognizes dihydro-orotic and converts it to orotic acid. Since there already exists a nucleotide sequence that encodes the former enzyme, a duplicate copy of that sequence is the best candidate for a modified sequence that encodes the second enzyme. This process, called evolution by gene duplication and divergence, is a well-documented phenomenon. It is much more efficient than discovering a sequence to encode a second enzyme from scratch.

One of the strengths of this kind of model building is that the predictions following from the models are testable. In the present case, the enzymes that catalyze the last two reactions in the synthesis of pyrimidines are predicted to have related amino acid sequences. There is a classical treatment of the subject of gene duplication and divergence in a little book by Ohno (1971).

The emergence of the first step in a pathway—in the present example, the conversion of orotic acid to uracil—also establishes an evolutionary tension. It creates a commitment that the second step—here, the conversion of dihydroorotic acid to orotic acid—serve the first. In other words, given that the first step is orotic acid utilization, it is dictated that the second step be orotic acid production.

At the same time that the first step constrains the second step, it also enables the second step. Natural Selection could not see an advantage in the production of orotic acid unless orotic acid is already being utilized to good effect. In contrast, Natural Selection would detect a disadvantage in the production of orotic acid if it were gratuitous and therefore wasteful. It is inescapable that the second step only makes biological and evolutionary sense in the context of the existing first step.

The duality of evolutionary steps, simultaneously constrained and enabled by what has gone before, becomes a key consideration in Darwinian thought.[16] A useful new step in a biological pathway, or any other process, must build upon or serve the existing pathway or process, and can only do so by utilizing whatever resources happen to be available. In effect, Mother Nature recognizes the needs of the evolving system and also recognizes the available remedy. This is done, of course, by experimentation with newly encoded genetic information, and not with foresight.

It is not a large conceptual step to begin viewing this experimentation as a series of probes or assays of the environment, conducted each generation. Each evolutionary step is then a response to these assays. Since this process is iterative, it ultimately results in nothing less than an interpretation of the environment. The rationale that life is the equivalent of interpretation extends to all of biology.

The evolutionary experimentation we have outlined to this point was all done at the level of the single cell and unfolded over a three-billion-year period. We can now address the unicellular-multicellular boundary and inquire what evolutionary breakthroughs made possible the transition to multicellular life. It remains our goal to identify and comprehend the factors that produced the Cambrian explosion.

In an ideal world, we would be able to study organisms that participated in the crossing of this boundary and, for comparative purposes, their contemporaries that did not. In the biological world to which we have access, we can apparently come awfully close to this ideal. Not only are there single-celled organisms in existence, but some surviving multicellular species are morphologically little different from their Cambrian ancestors. Of all such species, the sponges may be the most informative. As we will see, the simplest modern sponges can be

128

treated as if they witnessed the Cambrian explosion—sponges predated the explosion so were present for it, but were not participants in it. As witnesses, they have much to tell, provided that they have kept good records. Their records, of course, are their genes. Since the sponges have not changed much, not only in morphology but also in habitat, we infer that they have also changed little genetically, and therefore provide us with a real window on history.

Although the sponges that were present at the time of the Cambrian explosion were eukaryotic organisms, we should note in passing that the genetic content or complexity of a sponge cell is relatively small. As a frame of reference, consider the genetic complement of a fruit fly, which consists of about five thousand genes. The simpler sponge contains perhaps two or three thousand genes.

You will recall that we made a rough estimate that a trillion large molecules are required to duplicate a human cell. An insect cell might need only a tenth of that, or about 100 billion molecules. Suppose, in turn, that a sponge cell requires only a tenth the amount for an insect. In this very conservative scenario, the proliferation of a sponge cell would nonetheless require ten billion subunits of nucleotide bases, amino acids, phospholipids and other such molecules. In other words, the metabolic requirements of our simplest brethren are still measured on an astronomical scale. Let us be very clear about the point of this. The sponges that witnessed the Cambrian explosion were comprised of extremely ordered and complex cells.

Moreover, sponges were not simple colonies of similar cells. Instead, they were then, and are still, comprised of a variety of different cell types engaged in a rich variety of biological functions. Since an individual sponge, like a fly or a human, begins its existence as a single cell, that single cell must proliferate to generate the multicellular state, and its descendants must differentiate into the various cell types that comprise the adult. In this respect, the sponges are fully modern organisms.

In spite of the fact that the differentiation of cells during development is a subject with many unanswered questions, we can outline a general picture with complete confidence. It is quite clear, for example, that the behavior of a particular cell is a function of its position within the developing organism. Each cell recognizes where it is in the organism and responds by adjusting its genetic activity. That is, the fate of a cell is a function of selective gene expression. Depending upon the circumstances of the cell being observed, it may inactivate the expression of a particular set of genes, activate the expression of certain other genes or use some combination of activation and inactivation. The resulting pattern of expression, usually called differential gene activity, is what distinguishes the different cell types from each other. You may recall, from our outline of the Central Dogma, that gene expression is initiated from a part of the gene called its promoter. Differential gene expression is made possible by controlling access to promoters, and this accessibility is a function of complex sets of molecular recognitions. A bit later, we will review specific instances of promoter recognition.

The capacity for differential gene activity, and thus for the emergence of multicellular organisms with different types of cells, is clearly a central component of the Cambrian explosion. But differential gene activity is another name for the phenomenon of gene regulation, a genetic idea that was invented by prokaryotic cells long before the Cambrian era. It is of especial interest in the present context that striking examples of gene activation and inactivation are known in modern single cell eukaryotes. We can safely assert that differential gene activity, essential for the organisms of the Cambrian explosion, was invented by their single-celled ancestors and adapted for use in cell differentiation of multicellular descendants. Sponges, our chosen witnesses to the explosion, were themselves making use of differential gene activity as they watched the explosion occur. The invention of differential gene activity was a precondition for, and not a product of, the Cambrian explosion.

Although sponges are relatively simple organisms, they contain an impressive array of cell types. The exterior surface of a sponge consists of a cell layer like an epithelium or a skin. The cells of this layer tend to be flattened and contiguous over the entire surface. At the point of attachment of the sponge to its substratum, the epithelial cells form a basal lamina. The lamina is a sheet of extracellular adhesive material that plays a role in attachment; in organisms like ourselves, chemically similar laminae serve to bind cells like those of our skin (epithelium) to the connective tissues below.

The exterior of a sponge is interrupted by pore cells that connect the exterior to the hollow core (a simple sponge can be visualized as a thick-walled tube, closed at the bottom, with occasional perforations in the wall). Associated with pore cells are myocytes, contractile cells the regulate the pores' opening. The structure and function of myocytes is reminiscent of our own smooth muscle cells.

The interior surface of a sponge is largely a continuous array of cells called choanocytes; these cells bear a flagellum with which they create a flow of water that exits the sponge through an opening (osculum) in the top of the tube. Water enters the tube through the pores described above. Food particles, such as single-celled organisms suspended in the current of water created by the beating flagella, are trapped on the sticky surface of the choanocytes and ingested by an enfolding of the cell membrane (a process called phagocytosis). The structure of the sponge flagellum is identical to the flagellum that propels the sperm of all animals and to the cilia that create the flow of mucus that removes foreign particles from your trachea. The eukaryotic flagellum is another example of something invented once (bacterial flagella are different).

Between the exterior epithelium and the interior choanocytes is an interstitial space inhabited by a variety of cells types referred to collectively as amoebocytes. These are motile cells named after *amoebae*, free-living, single-celled organisms that are common inhabitants of ponds, moist soils and some marine habitats. Sponge amoebocytes are so-called because they move about the interstitial space *via* amoeboid motion, a complex process that involves building new cell membrane at the leading edge of the cell (i.e., in the direction of movement). Material for this construction is obtained by disassembling membrane at the trailing edge. In short, movement is achieved by adding to the front end and subtracting from the rear end. Certain human cell types—white blood cells, for example—move throughout the interstitial spaces in our bodies by the same mechanism. They congregate at sites of inflammation where they perform important functions of the immune system. If you have a site of inflammation anywhere on your body, white cells are this minute crawling to the rescue. You are inhabited by your own amoebocytes in much the same way that sponges are inhabited by theirs.

In sponges, one of the functions of amoebocytes is the receipt of foodstuffs from the choanocytes and its transportation to other amoebocytes within the interstitial space and to the epithelial cells lying across the space. Another variety of amoebocyte participates in the construction of a skeletal system which may contain either silicon-based or calcium-based structures of varying complexity, depending upon the species. Amoebocytes in the latter role are more appropriately seen as analogous to our own bone-forming osteocytes than as homologous to them.

Yet another class of amoebocyte secretes a fibrous, collagen-like material that gives additional strength to the sponge body through its role as a connective tissue. True collagen can be found playing a similar role in tissues like mammalian skin, for example.

The last cell types of sponges we will consider are those associated with sexual reproduction. It may at first seem odd that sponges are sexual organisms but they surely are by the rigorous criterion of being diploid organisms that arise by the union of haploid gametes. Although sponges are a diverse group, displaying an array of reproductive detail, their strategy is a general one. Their sperm—in enormous quantities—are discharged from the sponge body through the osculum and diffuse passively into the surrounding water.

In some species, a sperm that encounters an adult is actively taken up and transported to an egg within the interstitial space. The egg is a true egg, a

134

large cell packed with nutrients that will support early development of the sponge larva. The larva is also a true larva; union of the haploid sperm nucleus with the haploid egg nucleus produces a diploid zygotic nucleus within the single egg cell. Subsequent mitotic divisions of this cell, and the following divisions of its daughter cells and their descendants, produce a multicellular larva which is then discharged from the adult in a sort of rudimentary live birth. The discharged larva, if successful, will attach to a suitable substrate and continue developing into a new adult sponge. When this new sponge produces its own gametes, a cycle of life is completed.

With this overview of the cells of sponges in hand, let us return for a moment to consider a stationary choanocyte with its flagellum and the motile, flagellum-less amoebocyte. These two cells are genetically identical, having arisen by mitotic divisions from the single-celled zygote, produced by fusion of a sponge sperm with a sponge egg. By way of differential gene activity, the array of genes expressed in the choanocytes is different from the array expressed in the amoebocytes. Since the sponges were witnesses to the Cambrian explosion, we reiterate the conclusion that the art of differential gene activity––that is, gene regulation––was a forerunner of the landmark events of the Cambrian. We find reinforcement of the view that differential gene activity predates the Cambrian by reference to organisms even more simple than sponges. Consider the single-celled, free-living organism called *Naegleria* (reviewed by Fulton, 1977). *Naegleria* exists in moist soil as an amoeba, crawling here and there, engulfing such things as bacterial cells for its nutrition. However, with the onset of rain, *Naegleria* may abandon its amoeboid life style, produce a pair of flagella and swim away. When the rains subside and the environment is once again merely moist, *Naegleria* reverts to its amoeboid form.

Although *Naegleria*, like sponges, has both amoeboid and flagellated potential, the rules of engagement are quite different. In sponges, the decision whether to be amoeboid or flagellated is based upon environmental cues that reflect the cell's position within the sponge. We can say that genetically identical sponge cells differ across space. *Naegleria* responds to cues from a changing external environment. A single *Naegleria* cell (which remains genetically identical) has the capacity to differ across time.

One of the central biological innovations that distinguishes the developmental potential of a sponge, varying across space, from that of *Naegleria*, varying across time, is a re-ordering of the signals to which the cells respond. *Naegleria* reads signals from the inanimate world and responds to this assessment of things that are not self through differential gene activity. *Naegleria* adapts.

In contrast, sponge cells engage in an assessment of self and respond to this assessment through differential gene activity. Reading information about self has become substituted for reading information about the external environment. Thus, although a sponge is an array of genetically identical sister cells, these cells come to be physiologically distinguished from each other. Sponges develop.

The distinction between adaptation and development carries over to organisms like ourselves. The amoeboid cells of our immune system and the flagellated cells of our respiratory tract are behaving much more sponge-like than *Naegleria*-like. This transfer of function—assessment of internal factors being substituted for assessment of external factors— was a precondition for the emergence of complex multicellular organisms. The cells of such organisms must recognize each other.

The possession, by sponges, of differential gene activity, sexual reproduction and the capacity of cells to recognize each other tells us that each of these inventions predate the Cambrian explosion. We can now narrow the focus of our inquiry about the nature of the Cambrian explosion. Was it a Darwinian event, in which some relatively minor evolutionary invention created the appearance of great change by tying together a constellation of earlier inventions? Or was it, instead, a Punctuation in which some massive genetic revolution generated a change more profound than just appearances? With differential gene activity, sexual reproduction and cell-cell recognition already on the scene before the explosion, we will have to look beyond them for the key, or keys, to the sudden and simultaneous appearance of the ancestors of all modern fauna.

Earlier, we reviewed some of the components of cell division by which genetic information is transmitted from one generation to the next and, thus, by which like begets like. That review was focused at the level of genes themselves and, taking account of their mutability, we revised the conventional wisdom to the more modern and accurate view that like begets approximately like. While this property of life was necessarily present from its very origins, the advent of sexual reproduction gave it additional breadth and depth. Indeed, sexual reproduction added an entirely new dimension to the distribution of genetic variation and created a new vehicle for genetic expression.

The new dimension arises from the sexually driven phenomenon of recombining or shuffling genes. An asexual species can only create new varieties sequentially or linearly. A given individual can divide mitotically (or by fission in the case of bacteria) and produce two daughter cells, either of which may differ from its single parent by any variation that happened to be generated during the preceding round of replication and division. The new offspring, with any new variation, can only add additional variation in subsequent generations by iteration of this process. Equally importantly, any variant with deleterious effects is carried along as baggage. It can only be eliminated through the occurrence of events which specifically reverse or suppress its deleterious effects.

In contrast, sexual reproduction allows parallel creation of variants. Although individual variants arise by the same mutational processes in both sexual and asexual lineages, only in sexual systems can a new variant from one individual be brought together with a new variant from a second. Moreover, the same recombination or shuffling process that allows beneficial variants from different individuals to be incorporated into one lineage can simultaneously eliminate or "shuffle out" any deleterious variation. We must point out that the process is not directed. Instead, organisms produce enormous numbers of offspring amongst whom Natural Selection watches for favorable combinations of the variant genetic information.

The combined effects of variant creation, sexual shuffling of variation and the subsequent scrutiny of these genetic combinations by Natural Selection increase the capacity to cast off the unworkable, retain the well-suited and experiment with the new. This is exactly the stuff of Darwinian evolution.

If the advent of sex added new dimension to reproduction through the agency of recombination, it added an entirely new opportunity through the invention of the egg. The egg, of course, is a specialized gamete. We have already established that the invention of gametes predates the Cambrian explosion. We will argue here that multicellular life, of the sort represented in the Cambrian explosion, only became possible when one of those early gametes became an egg, making the invention of the egg a turning point in evolution. The story of that invention is a circuitous one—although eggs are end products of meiotic, gamete producing division, the journey began with the invention of mitosis, the asexual mechanism by which cells normally proliferate.

Mitotic division occurs in essentially three steps (Appendix 2). The chromosomes replicate, the two copies (daughters) of each chromosome separate from each other and the two resulting nuclei are partitioned into two daughter cells. This scheme of division works equally well for both haploid and diploid nuclei, since each chromosome in the dividing nucleus replicates and separates independently from all other chromosomes in the nucleus.

Meiosis differs from mitosis in two fundamental ways. The first of these is that the events of meiosis, unlike those of mitosis, require the diploid state. Following chromosome replication, in a cell committed to dividing meiotically, the chromosomes form very specific pairs based upon homology. That is, each chromosome recognizes and

140

pairs with the only other chromosome in the nucleus that carries the same genetic information (remembering that these chromosomes are very similar but, because of mutation, are not identical). It is during this paired phase that homologous chromosomes can and do exchange pieces with each other (*via* crossingover, as described in Appendix 2). Then, in the first of the two divisions of meiosis, the paired homologs separate from each other. In mitosis, the two copies of each replicated chromosome separate from each other. The pairing of, crossingover between and separation of homologs can only occur in diploid cells.

The second major point of difference in meiosis is that, following the first division and the separation of homologs from each other, the two products divide again without the occurrence of chromosome replication. Aside from the omission of replication, the second division of meiosis proceeds exactly as a mitotic division of a haploid nucleus. In other words, the first meiotic division produces two haploid nuclei with their chromosomes pre-replicated and ready for mitotic division. This entry into division, in the absence of a proximal replication of chromosomes, is unique to the second meiotic division. The mitotic divisions of these latter two nuclei produce four haploid nuclei with chromosomes that are not replicated. It is haploid nuclei such as these that are partitioned off into cells and differentiated into sperm in males and eggs in females.

The invention of meiosis—and therefore of sex as we know it—was probably accomplished with a good deal of economy. Its emergence necessarily begins with a primitive (pre-Cambrian) population of haploid, single-celled, eukaryotic organisms. A billion years ago, more or less, these cells were already accomplished in the art of mitotic reproduction. A central part of their achievement was the discovery of a mechanism by which to control the cell division cycle. That mechanism couples the initiation of cell division to cell size. In effect, a proliferating cell grows until the ratio of total cellular volume to nuclear volume (the latter remains essentially constant) reaches a certain value. Reaching this value generates a signal to initiate DNA synthesis. Completion of replication is then a secondary signal that initiates the onset of division itself. Thus, a growth-replication-division cycle becomes a cause and effect cascade. Sufficient growth initiates duplication, completion of duplication initiates division and completion of division initiates the next round of growth.

A second component of the well-ordered mechanism of cell division is that which assures the inclusion of a complete set of the genetic information in both daughters. A dividing bacterial cell apparently achieves this end through the attachment of its chromosome to the cell membrane. Following chromosome duplication, the attachment site splits and the halves, each bearing a daughter chromosome,

142

move apart or are driven apart by the occurrence of membrane growth between them.

The mechanism of chromosome separation in early eukaryotes was probably similar to that of bacteria except that the function had been moved from the exterior cell membrane to the internalized nuclear membrane. (In modern eukaryotic cell division, chromosomes move apart on fibers that connect to a special region of the chromosome called the centromere or kinetochore. The kinetochore is presumably the vestige of the primitive membrane attachment site.) In any event, a billion years ago, the seas were teeming with single haploid cells that grew, replicated their chromosomes and separated the daughter chromosomes by separating the chromosomal attachment sites.

The transition from a biosphere of haploid cells reproducing mitotically (asexually) to one in which there are also diploid cells reproducing meiotically (sexually) requires a set of inventions. It was necessary to invent diploidy. It was necessary to invent meiosis (in order to convert diploid cells back to haploid cells) and it was necessary to invent cell fusion (in order to restore diploidy).

A layperson looking at this set of requirements might conclude that the sequence of inventions would have to put cell fusion first, since this is required for the creation of diploidy, which, in turn, is required for the creation of meiosis. Biologists, in contrast, might hesitate to draw this conclusion because they are encumbered with the knowledge that diploidy can also be generated internally by any one of several mechanisms known collectively as endoreduplication. However, we will ignore endoreduplication and follow the instincts of the layperson for two reasons.

In the first place, the invention of meiosis in response to endoreduplication would seem to imply a meiosis-endoreduplication cycle–a cycle that exists nowhere in nature. On the other hand, the invention of meiosis in response to cell fusion implies a meiosis-fusion loop––a phenomenon that is well known indeed. Secondly, we will see that the invention of cell fusion may have done more than make meiosis possible. Meiosis may have been inevitable.

We know at least three mechanisms by which fusion can occur between modern cells. One is a virus-mediated process in which a virus particle simultaneously binds to two cells, essentially creating a tube that connects them, and this resolves into a complete union of the two cell membranes. A second mechanism involves special pore-like inclusions (ionosphores) in membranes that can mediate union of two membranes in contact with each other.

The third mechanism of cell fusion—the one most likely relevant to our topic—utilizes a class of protein molecules called fusogens. This type of protein is located on sperm heads, for example, and allows them to fuse with the egg membrane. The action of a fusogenic protein essentially reverses the process of daughter cells pinching off from each other

144

at the end of cell division, and this may provide some clue to their origin. Evolution by duplication and divergence of a gene encoding a "pinching" function comes to mind.

What behavior would we expect of haploid cells that have acquired the capacity to fuse with each other? The first consequence of fusion would be the production of one cell containing two nuclei. A cell of this type is called a heterokaryon. If the two nuclei fuse, we have the invention of the diploid state. We propose that diploidy was ultimately invented in this manner, but that a stable diploid state required another step. In other words, the diploid cell that was produced by the first cell fusion was inherently unstable in a very particular way.

The suspicion that the first diploids were unstable is based upon several observations about the behavior of chromosomes in cell division. The first of these is that the nucleus and its chromosome(s) have a special orientation with respect to the rest of the cell. In the primitive diploid, twice the number of chromosomes suddenly found themselves needing to occupy this place of orientation simultaneously. The cell, with its haploid heritage, had no prior experience with this arrangement.

At this point, we propose the specific property that the fusion of nuclei was at least related to, and possibly mediated by, the sites at which chromosomes attached to the nuclear membrane (for ease of argument, we will assume that each of the fusing haploid nuclei possessed a single chromosome. The fusion product, therefore, contained a single pair of chromosomes). The consequence of the properties and behavior of the attachment sites was that they came to sit adjacent to each other on the nuclear membrane. This condition would follow from the likelihood that there was normally but a single place for an attachment site to reside, so each of the two attachment sites would have to be there.[17]

The ancient diploid cell, created by the fusion outlined above, would have grown until it attained the proper size for division. Since it contained two chromosomes, it would need to attain twice the cell volume of its haploid progenitors. Upon reaching that volume, chromosome replication would have begun. The end of replication would have signaled the next step in the cascade, the division of the nucleus and cell. This presented the cell with the first of the things it had not seen before—two attachment sites occupying the place in the division machinery that had been designed for a single attachment.

Under normal (haploid) circumstances for these primitive cells, the single attachment site of a haploid cell would have sat on the midline of the axis of division. If, in the prototype diploid cells, the two attachment sites attempted to occupy that site simultaneously, they would end up straddling the midline, and the primitive mechanism for separating the attachment sites would have fallen between them. A schematic of this model is pictured below.

146

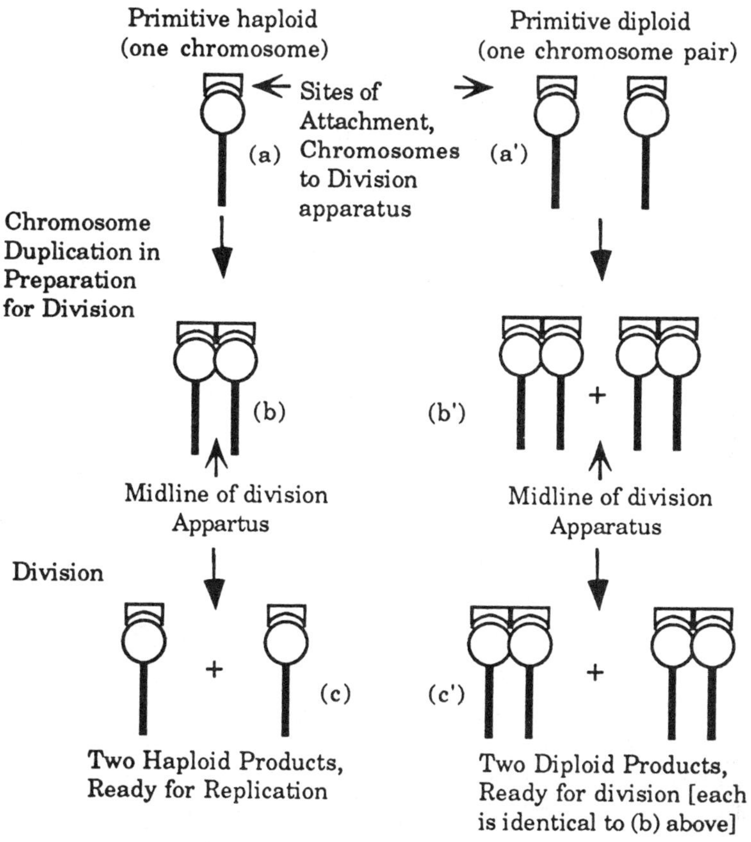

The ensuing cell division in the diploid would then separate the attachment sites and thus the homologous chromosomes, and is therefore equivalent to the first meiotic division: it creates two daughter cells, both of which have received a single, replicated chromosome.

The condition of these daughters would have been a pre-Cambrian surprise. To the primitive cell division machinery, the size and chromosome content of these cells would appear to be that of haploid cells that had grown to maturity and replicated their chromosomes. In the cascade system of mitotic cell division, these cells are ready to divide mitotically. That is, a second cell division would occur without a proximate replication of chromosomes, concluding a sequence of events that constitutes a primitive meiosis.

The invention of stable diploidy from these beginnings requires only that the first division of the meiotic sequence be suppressed. This could be accomplished, for example, by rotating the pair of homologous attachment sites about their axis of symmetry so that they sit on a line perpendicular to the direction of division.[18] The plane of division in this nucleus would then pass through each attachment site, as it did in mitosis in the haploid progenitor of these primitive diploids, rather than between the two homologous attachment sites. Division would then generate a pair of diploid daughter cells. Furthermore, the chromosomes in these cells would be recognized as having divided and the ratio of nuclear to total cell volume would be appropriate to the divided state. Thus, the next act of these cells would be a round of growth, followed by chromosome replication and another cell division. The sequence of the inventions leading to modern

148

sexual reproduction would thus be (1) haploid mitosis, followed by (2) cell fusion, then by (3) diploid meiosis, and lastly by (4) diploid mitosis.[19]

It is a prediction of this model of diploid mitosis that the function suppressing the first meiotic division—we used the possibility of rotating the attachment sites—be an added function as opposed to a modified function. In this way, cells could evolve regulatory control of this function that enables them to turn the function off. The ability to control expression versus non-expression of the function allows the cell to be mitotic or meiotic as a regulatory response to its environment. All modern eukaryotes regulate their sexual cycles in just this way. That is, they are diploid cells that enter meiosis under certain environmental conditions. It is provocative that some fungi, among them the extensively studied *Neurospora crassa*, enter meiosis immediately upon achieving the diploid state, as if diploidy remains an unstable condition for these organisms. Indeed, Neurospora has no non-sexual diploid phase. If such diploidy is created experimentally, it rapidly breaks down to haploidy *via* quasi-meiotic chromosome behavior during subsequent cell divisions.

At first glance, the model presented here seems to contradict the classical view that meiosis is a derivative of mitosis. In fact, the model actually strings two aberrant mitotic division together. The first division of the proposed primitive meiosis is an aberrant mitosis in that it invokes aberrant behavior of attachment sites in an otherwise wholly mitotic apparatus. The second division is an aberrant mitosis in that it proceeds in a wholly mitotic fashion upon the proper mitosis-based assessment that replication of chromosomes has been completed, although no proximate replication occurred.

What the model does revise is our view of the relationship of diploidy to meiosis. We grew up learning, in essence, that meiosis reduces diploid cells to haploid cells: i.e., meiosis eliminates diploidy, whereas the model here contends that diploidy arose as the suppression of meiosis: i.e., that diploidy is the elimination of meiosis, the accidental consequence of cells learning to recognize each other and fuse.

An arcane model for the evolution of meiosis may seem far afield from an exploration of the meaning of life. What the model leads us to see, however, is that the interrelations between haploidy, diploidy and meiosis comprise the invention of an exploratory cycle. In this cycle, diploid cells became the means for their haploid progenitors to begin exploring multicellular life styles. A diploid, multicellular experiment can report its success to the next generation, and simultaneously experiment with genetic variations of its success, by employing the meiotic return to haploidy. That is, diploid cells can explore multicellular existence precisely because they can escape it. The iteration of this cycle is an evolutionary ratchet of unprecedented power. The

150

sexual life cycle, the emergent manifestation of exploration and escape, was thus a fundamental precursor of the Cambrian explosion. However, two additional inventions had to make their appearances before the Cambrian explosion could occur. One of these is a variation on the theme of cell-cell recognition. Multicellular life is absolutely dependent upon the type of cell recognition that is accompanied by adhesion rather than fusion. The second necessary invention, as promised earlier, is the egg.

An adult human consists of about a hundred thousand billion cells of about 200 different types. Under normal circumstances, each of these billions of cells is in the right place at the right time. The production of this remarkable complexity is achieved through the expression of a refined developmental pathway built upon a simple, repeating theme. Cells send signals to each other and receive signals from each other. Different cells, as a consequence of occupying different positions, receive different signals. Different signals elicit different cellular responses and behaviors. In a sense, the system is analogous to a set of scripted conversations in which the participants talk and listen carefully. The language is that of the genetic code. The four billion year old dialog is ever experimental.

The first step in development, from a fertilized egg containing a single nucleus, is a series of cell divisions that produce the early embryo. What at first seems little more than a simple cluster of cells is, in fact, a set of cells that have already begun to behave differently from each other. They do this as a function of their positions within the cluster. Cells can sense their positions because (1) different positions are chemically different and (2) the cells are equipped to monitor and respond to these chemical differences. Iterations of recognition and response generate functionally distinct groups of cells, ultimately giving rise to cells as diverse as the neurons that transmit electrical impulses and contain our thoughts, the osteoblasts that build bone, the lymphocytes that display and secrete antibodies, and a host of epithelial cells that line everything from our exterior boundaries to our stomachs. All of these cell types contain exactly the same genetic information, but are expressing different parts of it.

A good deal of the machinery that allows cells to monitor their immediate environments is located in the cell membrane. In a manner of speaking, cells can feel, taste and see their positions through membrane-bound receptors of environmental cues. The properties of cell membranes that mediate the system of cue recognition and genetic response, particularly the membrane proteins embedded in and attached to these membranes, constitute one of the most complex systems in all of biology. They, and the genes that encode them are at the very core of the differences between a single-celled amoeba and an elephant.

Since the membrane is the boundary between a cell and its environment, including other cells, it is not surprising that mechanisms for recognizing features of the environment, including self *versus* non-self, should be located there. For example, most of the major reactions of vertebrate immune response occur at cell membranes. It is one of the modern biological ironies, and horrors, that Human Immunodeficiency Virus, HIV, recognizes a component of the cell membrane in a critical class of cells of the immune system. By infecting these cells, HIV ultimately dismantles the very biological system that would otherwise fight the viral infection and the associated secondary infections that lead to lethality. In other words, the membrane components that make certain cells immuno-active, in the presence of HIV, become viral targets.

The rejection of tissue and organ transplants and the interactions between cells in the development of multicellular organisms are also membrane mediated phenomena. The special types of cell-cell recognitions seen in development and immune response are properties of multicellular but not unicellular species. The invention of such capacities for recognition was a necessary bridge to the Cambrian explosion.

Some types of membrane mediated recognition events are common to both unicellular and multicellular organisms. For example, amoeboid single cells and the white blood cells distributed throughout vertebrate bodies can engulf bacterial cells by first recognizing them, drawing them into an invagination generated in the cell membrane and then internalizing that invagination as an intracellular vesicle. Inside the cell, the vesicle fuses with another vesicle, a lysosome filled with digestive enzymes, and the engulfed bacteria are destroyed. An amoeba does this as a form of feeding. White cells do it as part of the multicellular organism's defenses against pathogens. Same process, different application.

As mentioned earlier, unicellular and multicellular organisms also share the cell-cell recognition associated with cell fusion and sexual reproduction. Since sexual reproduction must predate multicellular life, at least in the major diploid lineages, the cell-cell recognitions that occurred during the first unions of haploid cells occupy a special place in life's history. One might argue that, transitorily at least, these were two-celled organisms and thus the first multicelled organisms. In any event, the first components of self recognition were invented by single cells. Otherwise, the first recognitions could not have occurred and existing multicellular life would not have evolved.

The earliest experimental evidence for the existence of cell-cell recognition came from studies done with sponges. When an individual sponge is mechanically or enzymatically disrupted into single cells, and these cells are allowed to sit in the bottom of a dish filled with sea water, the cells begin to migrate,

154

to form clusters, and these clusters form new sponges. When cells from different species of sponges are mixed under these conditions, they form separate sponges, each containing only cells of one species and not the other. More recently, such experiments have been done with tissues from frogs and mice. Not only do the cells from these systems reaggregate, but the individual cell types remember where they belong within the tissue.

Although life was invented as molecular recognition at the level of the central dogma, it began to see its full potential with the invention of recognition at the level of cell membranes. Cell membranes have become biological mirrors, reflecting to the outside what the cell is and reflecting the outside world inward, telling the cell where it is and what surrounds it The cell is recognized and recognizes by way of the signals and sensors embedded in its membrane.

Our treatment of cell and molecular biology, as modest as it is, has nonetheless allowed us to trace an outline of evolution up to the point at which it poised itself to begin its explosive experimentation, and success, with multicellular existence. Life arrived at this threshold on the strength of four categories of discovery. The first is, and always will be, life's signal achievement, the single cell—including its capacity to capture and transfer energy, its capacity to synthesize organic molecules and its capacity to store and replicate all of its acquired knowledge about survival on earth. This acquired knowledge is stored in its DNA, its panoply of genes.

The second discovery, on top of this core chemistry, is the art of adaptation through differential gene activity. The same cell can have very different behaviors depending upon where it finds itself. Cells began to learn the art of recognizing and interpreting their environments. Successful genes are historical records of the accurate recognition and truthful interpretation of those environments.

The single cell turned another corner when it supplemented the ability to read its environment with the capability of recognizing those instances when the thing it was seeing (or feeling or tasting) in its environment was itself. Single cells began to interpret themselves (I am compelled to use the phrase "birth of cell consciousness" so that certain individuals of my acquaintance will be sure to groan). In the first instance, this discovery of self recognition set the stage for sexuality *via* cell fusion. The advent of sexuality, by virtue of its heightened capacity to shuffle genetic information, evidently marks an increase in the real rate of evolution (the rate measured per generation). You will recall that new genetic combinations are produced sequentially by asexual reproduction, but that variation produced in parallel, in different cell lineages, can be combined in a geometric fashion by sexual reproduction. The conversion from asexual to sexual reproduction involves a change in life style beyond the obvious interactions between cells—by virtue of these interactions, cells could abandon their passive approach and begin actively to probe their environments with combinations of characteristics from disparate sources.

One of the new ways that cells could begin to probe their environments was by expressing their repertory of behaviors in a cooperative fashion with their fellows. Suppose a type of cell has learned the capacity to exist as either a feeding amoeba or a swimming flagellate, as in the case of *Naegleria* discussed earlier. If it could find a way to link itself together as two cells, it would have instant ability to test a new environment in which to live. It would double in size and presumably be harder for something else to eat. In addition, it would create the opportunity for one of its cells to remain in feeding mode while the other was in swimming mode. It could swim and feed simultaneously. If such a niche existed—one in which simultaneous swimming and feeding were advantageous—the first two-celled swimming and eating creature would be uniquely qualified to occupy it. But it would have a problem to solve. It would have to have some reliable mechanism by which the two cells could make the decision that each would undertake a different labor. This is the invention that brings us back to the egg.

Eggs carry out two essential functions in those organisms evolutionarily committed to reproduction *via* sperm and egg. In the first place, they are large cells and provide nourishment for the early (cleavage) divisions of the diploid nucleus following the union of the haploid sperm and egg nuclei. Secondly, and the point most relevant to the quandary of the two cells that must decide which is to feed and which is to swim, eggs are packaged with information that prompts such decisions.

Imagine that the egg of the two-celled organism we are considering contains a substance, at just one end of the egg, that induces a cell in its presence to abandon the amoeboid (feeding) life style in favor of a flagellated (swimming) life style. Development of the two-celled adult from such an egg would be a very regular process. Following fertilization, the newly formed zygote would divide once to produce the two cells of the adult. One of these cells would be free of the inducing substance and thus remain amoeboid. The other cell would be in contact with the inducing substance and thus become flagellated. A two-celled system of this sort would be the simplest possible case of morphogenesis—the process by which different parts of an organism take on different forms and functions.

In the real world of biology, we are more apt to be speaking of the morphogenesis of grander things like nervous systems, livers and skeletal muscle. But even in something as complex as a mammal, the initial steps in development involve the partitioning of cells into distinct groupings that will have distinct

158

fates. The instructions that route cells into their fates are expressed at the very outset of development—in fact, in the best studied systems, they are known to be laid down in the egg during its manufacture, predating fertilization. Thus, developmental decision-making begins with the first cell divisions in the fertilized egg.

The substances that carry these bits of developmental information are called morphogens. Without them, complex morphogenesis cannot occur and, without them, the Cambrian explosion would not have occurred. Since the Cambrian explosion represents the appearance of morphogen-based development, morphogens necessarily predated the explosion. In other words, the embryological complexity of the post-Cambrian organisms had to have had its source in an ancestor that was embryologically more simple. When this logic is followed to its origins, it inevitably leads us back to the first egg or egg-like cell. Once again, we see that all of the preconditions for the invention of the egg, and therefore for the occurrence of the Cambrian explosion, were necessarily laid down by single-celled organisms and their simplest pre-Cambrian multicellular derivatives.

We noted earlier that eggs play the dual roles of providing both nourishment and developmental information for the early embryo, and intimated that the information is placed in the egg asymmetrically.

159

Imagine a morphogen that establishes the front-to-back (anterior-posterior) axis of the embryo as being placed at some point just inside the cell membrane of the egg. Now traverse the periphery of the egg through a one-quarter turn and place a morphogen that establishes the top-to-bottom (dorsal-ventral) axis of the embryo. The embryo that begins to develop when this egg is fertilized will have a head and a tail (the latter is not-the-head) and a top and a bottom (not-the-top). It also, one might say free of charge, has a right and a left. In other words, the introduction of a small number of innovations establishes the potential for profound biological shape. Embryos emerging from eggs packed with such anterior-posterior, dorsal-ventral information are more than just balls of cells. However, their ability to respond to this information requires that there also exist a system for reading the information.

The system that reads the developmental information packed into the egg is, as we would suspect, comprised of genes. The morphogens or developmental inducers packaged asymmetrically into eggs are molecules that bind to specific promoters on chromosomes of cells in contact with the morphogens, and activate the genes expressed from those promoters. In other words, egg-borne morphogens cause cells to become distinguished from each other by inducing specific cases of differential gene activity. These first acts of differentiation are the first stages in a cascade of differential gene activity that comes to distinguish one type of cell from another in the adult.

The functioning of a cascade can be illustrated by elaborating on the model of the two-celled organism we used above. The developmental program of that organism—amoeboid cell plus morphogen-induced flagellated cell—can be revised so that its first cell division is supplemented with an additional command: if you are an amoeboid cell in contact only with a flagellated cell, divide again. The resulting cascade consists of the sequence in which the morphogen induces creation of a flagellated cell, the presence of which then induces the non-flagellated cell to divide again.

Whereas the two-celled organism consisting of an amoeboid cell plus a flagellated cell arose from the simplest imaginable act of morphogenesis, the three-celled organism described here is the product of the simplest imaginable morphogenetic cascade. It is precisely by such cascades that development of biological complexity occurs—a stimulus has a consequence that becomes a secondary stimulus with an additional consequence. The cascade metaphor applies because each added consequence in the cascade is downstream in the series of events. Furthermore, the system flows in one direction, a little as if it were under biology's equivalent of gravitational pull.

The seemingly tripartite system of development (in which part one is the manufacture of egg-borne morphogenic substances, part two is the ability to read morphogens and part three is the set of secondary cascades) on closer inspection appears to have a fourth part. This is implied by the need for a mechanism to place morphogens into the egg in the characteristic, asymmetric fashion.

The mechanisms by which morphogens, once manufactured, are distributed in eggs are quite variable and notable in their own right. Typically, the egg is attended by a number of other cells during its development. These other cells, called nurse cells in many systems, produce a variety of components, including energy sources, components of the biosynthetic machinery, building blocks—and morphogens for export into the egg. You might think of the egg as a balloon being inflated simultaneously from a number of directions. Once fully "inflated," the egg is ready for fertilization.

It is worthwhile to remind ourselves here that the egg and its attending nurse cells are themselves distinct from other cells by virtue of differential gene activity. Their mode of differentiation is a consequence of the particular developmental cascade within which their progenitor cells became included. The developmental cycle initiated by the egg-borne morphogens thus comes back full circle to the elaboration of more eggs packaged with morphogens. This full circle is called an organism's life cycle, a concise if bland description of a remarkable system.

162

The complexity of the life cycle from fertilized egg to adult and back to egg again is so complex, and we are giving it such short shrift, that it merits at least a brief reiteration.

•The union of a haploid egg with a haploid sperm generates a diploid zygote. The single cell of the zygote divides mitotically to initiate development. The embryo increases in cell number through successive cell divisions.

•The cells of the embryo are genetically identical to each other but have location-specific differences in potential due to the asymmetrical distribution of morphogens within the egg.

•The asymmetry of the egg generates an asymmetrical embryo. Cells within the embryo begin to differ from each other physiologically through region-specific acts of differential gene activity. Once the egg-borne morphogens have induced an initial set of distinct cell types, these cells begin to interact with each other in a second tier of morphogenetic inductions.

•Any given cell, at any point in development, has a specific set of characteristics that reflects (1) what its mother cell was and (2) where it finds itself.

•One of these pathways of cell differentiation utilizes a hierarchy of cues to inform the cells at the path's end that they are eggs (or sperm), thus empowered to escape the diploid phase and complete the cycle by transmitting the findings of

the present generation to the next. The organisms
of the Cambrian explosion are direct descendants
of the ancestors who invented the pathway
leading to the informed egg.

If the egg is a chief architect of the Cambrian
explosion, it is also a chief architect of one of the great
misconceptions in biology—the widely held view,
however vague, that life is discontinuous. The highly
evolved life cycle consisting of egg to adult to egg
creates the illusion that birth is a miracle, as if life had
disappeared, only to be resurrected. In fact, the
miracle of birth is equally miraculous with the miracle
of gametogenesis, since each is absolutely essential for
the propagation of the cycle. Ironically, single-celled
organisms that nonetheless reproduce sexually
always stay small, so that the opportunity for an
illusion of discontinuity never presents itself.[20]
Indeed, the cure for the foible of the
discontinuity illusion is to focus on the single cells
that actually bridge the generations. Whether we look
to single-celled amoebae or elephants, the bridge
consists of single cells and nothing more. In their
exercise of sexual reproduction, both amoebae and
elephants make use of exactly two haploid gametes to
produce one diploid zygote. From that point, the
divergence is that elephants employ a more
complicated and expensive set of mechanisms to
prepare the next generation of haploid cells to bridge
to the next generation of elephants. The miracle of an

164

elephant's birth is no greater a part of the elephant continuum than the miracle of meiosis that produces elephant sperm and eggs. For elephants, as for amoebae, life has continuity only at the level of single cells. The extinction of elephants, should that ever come to pass, will be defined as the loss of continuity at that same level.

As much as we sometimes try, we cannot escape our single cell heritage, neither as species nor as individuals. We each began as single cells and our contribution to posterity can only occur as single cells. The converse of this, of course, is that the biological landscape, looking backwards in evolutionary time, is one from which our multicellular ancestors simply disappear, leaving only their unicellular progenitors for our admiration.

The illusion of discontinuity between generations, created by the life cycles of multicellular organisms, appears to lie at the heart of a more subtle ruse. This is the perception that multicellular life exploded onto the scene some 500 million years ago. The life-forms constituting that explosion appear to be discontinuous with everything that came before. In fact, however, they are not discontinuous with their progenitors. They are, instead, the first modern multicellular life cycles to be recorded in the fossil record and so give the appearance of a discontinuity. We now undertake to quibble—and we emphasize quibble—with Stephen J. Gould and his colleagues in the school of "punctuated equilibrium."

If we are to argue that the Cambrian explosion wasn't really an explosion, we will need to suggest what it was instead. In tracing some of the history of the single cell, we have seen that most of the inventions required for multicellular existence had to have predated the Cambrian. We have also seen that early dabblings in multicellular invention failed—the Ediacaron fauna, for example. However, it is a virtual cinch that something from the Ediacaron fauna, or something similar to that fauna, did in fact survive as foundation for the Cambrian fauna. The Ediacaron fauna, after all, had clearly made progress in the art of cell-cell recognition and adhesion. The Cambrian organisms added to this what was earlier referred to as profound shape. All profound biological shape is embryological in origin, and it always begins with an informative egg.

The egg system has certain parallels to the process of first writing and then reading an instruction manual. It consists of a set of instructions (specific gene products) being laid down (written) in the specialized egg cell as it is produced. These instructions are subsequently read by a second set of genes, beginning when cell division is reinstated by fertilization of the quiescent egg. The evolution of the capacity to "write" and "read" instructions traces back to single-celled organisms. They first invented the ability to respond to differences in the external

166

environment, then turned this invention inward, generating an internal system to which they could respond in a controlled and regular way. It is this invention of a controlled and regular response to one's own internal system of signals—the "ecosystem" of molecular gradients in the egg—that defines morphogenetic development and, therefore, the Cambrian explosion.

One powerful line of evidence for this proposition is surprisingly accessible. If we take a layman's tour through the Cambrian fauna recorded in the Burgess Shale, we see pre-Cambrian creatures like sponges but the stunning thing, and what is really meant by the Cambrian explosion, is the sudden appearance of animals, like those illustrated below, that were unlike anything seen before.

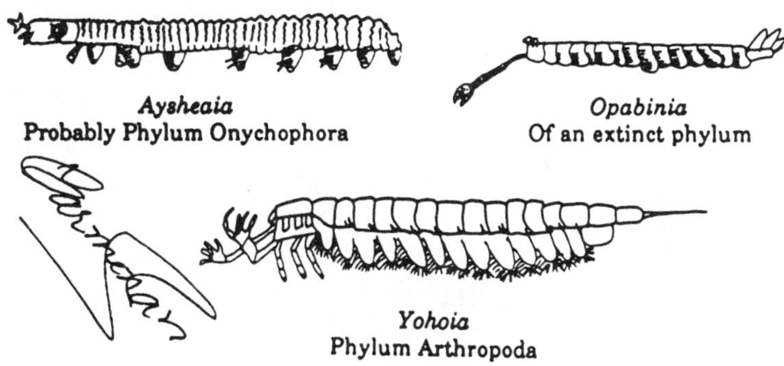

In addition to being new on the scene, these creatures have a second thing in common. They are all built of segments and this manner of building is inseparable from the egg. The bipartite information system, built into the egg, opened the door to wild experimentation with bodies composed of segments.[21]

There is now a large and rapidly growing literature on the subject of segments—one can find an introduction to this literature in virtually any modern text in biology, genetics, biochemistry or molecular biology. As a developmental phenomenon, segments arise from localized differences in cell differentiation induced by localized differences in gradients of substances we earlier referred to as morphogens. Modern organisms—from fruit flies to people—are highly segmented. Their development begins with the informational gradients in the egg and proceeds from there down a segmented path.

It remains the case that at the level of organisms, the Cambrian Explosion is aptly named. After some three billion years of single cells, every existing and a number of extinct animal phyla suddenly appeared, within a relatively brief window of time, at the beginning of the Cambrian period. But if we adhere more rigorously to a criterion of continuity—that is, keep our attention focused on the genetic changes associated with the explosion—the picture is quite different. At the level of the genome, all we need to propose is the addition of a small number of genetic innovations. These added genes were to have a profound effect on the history of life— they are not just any old genes. On the other hand,

168

the inventions of the genes encoding, say, the enzymes of pyrimidine biosynthesis were also to have a profound effect on life. Similarly, the discovery of meiosis had its own profound effects. If these inventions do not merit the title "explosion," then neither does the invention of the egg nor, for that matter, the invention of dinosaurs. At the level of genes, none of these phenomena constitutes evidence of an explosion. At the level of genes, they more closely fit a continuum. This is of no mean importance, since it is the information content of genes that changes over evolutionary time.

We will end this quibble with the idea of punctuated equilibrium on a metaphorical note. Suppose you noticed, from a distance, some human activity in a vacant field. After several days, the frame of a house suddenly appears and is quickly capped with a roof. The house appears to you to have exploded onto the scene. Your curiosity piqued, you cross the field to the actual site of the house and find that it sits on a foundation. You then realize that most of the work to this point had not been visible to you. Before the carpenters raised the frame and the roof, others had laid out and dug footings, placed reinforcing steel, installed plumbing lines and poured concrete foundation and slab. Erecting the frame on these beginnings is a little like the Cambrian explosion being built on the foundation of prior biological discoveries. There is much less explosion than meets the eye. I hope Charles Darwin would have liked this metaphor.

The invention of the bipartite genetic system of the egg lies at the center of another controversy, not just about eggs, but about sex itself. This controversy also leads us to our last visit to the idea of the selfish gene. On the question of sex, the idea that genes are selfish goes right over the edge.

One of the more surprising questions to be raised about sexual reproduction is this: why is it carried out by two sexes (as opposed to, say, three)? It is instructive to consider the origin of this question. It was posed by R. A. Fisher, the father of mathematical population genetics and something of an icon in the field. Fisher made the point that, as a question of mathematical theory, the usual condition of two sexes in a species of organism makes no particular sense. Apparently mesmerized by the considerable power of Fisher's mathematical modeling, some biologists may have confused his arithmetic with life itself.

A clear manifestation of this appeared several years ago in the form of a remarkable proposition that the existence of just two sexes in organisms like human beings is explained by selfish genes. (See, for example, the journal *Science* 17 July, 1992, page 324 for an admittedly elegant but arguably breathless exposition of this idea). The rationale for the evolution of two sexes, in the eyes of the selfish

170

geniteers, is rooted in intergenomic conflict management. The need for conflict management is seen to arise because the union of two gametes brings different copies of the genome into a common cytoplasm. When forced into a common cytoplasm, genes are imagined to attack each other. Thus, for example, genes contributed by a male parent (even if they came from his mother) will figuratively pull a knife on genes from a female parent (even if they came from her father), in order to increase the fitness of the male parent (the genes from the female parent are doing similarly unfriendly things). There are two sexes, the argument seems to go, because conflict management would be more difficult if there were three. The imagined need to quell intracellular genetic mayhem may be the most bizarre chapter in the selfish view of life.

There is an alternative and substantially less violent explanation for there being two sexes. In the course of each generation of metazoans like ourselves, if there is to be a subsequent generation, some subset of adults must submit eggs that will support the embryogenesis of that subsequent generation. Similarly, some subset of adults must submit sperm cells (or pollen cells in the case of plants). These relatively simple cells, by fertilizing eggs, simultaneously restore the diploid, adult genomic condition and initiate the embryogenesis of the next generation. The invention of this litany is what we see reflected in the Cambrian explosion. It is difficult to imagine Mother Nature, in her parsimonious splendor, troubling to invent three sexes to effect these two functions. For clarity, let us restate these functions:

1. Eggs are laid.
2. Eggs are fertilized.

Although the order of these events may vary, it requires exactly two sexes to achieve them. On the other hand, organisms without embryogenesis are not constrained to provide the embryogenesis-enabling function of the egg and the initiating function of the sperm. That is, such organisms have no sexes at all in that the partners contribute equally and symmetrically to sexual reproduction. It is precisely within these organisms, sexually reproducing but without sexes, that the selfish geniteers find their evidence for genomic conflict management.

The selfish geniteers also pose a second and related question—it is probably the more interesting question. Why is the sperm cell (or pollen grain) so small? These cell types typically deliver no more than a haploid nucleus to the recipient egg which provides all other cellular constituents. Among these constituents are such things as mitochondria, essentially little cellular powerhouses converting sugars into usable energy. Mitochondria, it turns out, contain their own little chromosomes. If both male and female gametes contributed mitochondria to the

172

zygote, it would contain diverse mitochondrial genomes. In fact, it is actually here that the selfish geniteers invoke the need for conflict management, imagining that the mitochondria would do battle. In devising this model, they ignore a good deal of mainstream literature.

In the fungus *Neurospora crassa*, for example, it is known that different strains of the organism will fuse in such a way that their haploid nuclei and mitochondria will happily share a common cytoplasm. The key feature of this arrangement, called a heterokaryon, is that the nuclei do not fuse. Thus, each maintains its own cell division apparatus, including the centrosomes which organize the mitotic spindle. Strains which behave in this way are said to be of the same mating type.

In sharp contrast, Neurospora unions between strains of opposite mating type—that is, sexual unions—combine the nucleus plus cytoplasm from one parent with just the nucleus from the other: i.e., one of the participants behaves as a male parent. Furthermore, either strain may assume either sexual role, the first to arrive at the scene of the union playing the role of female. Under these circumstances, the two nuclei must fuse and thus share a cell division apparatus. The simplest way to get both nuclei onto one division apparatus is to leave one copy of the apparatus behind at the moment of cell fusion. The simplest way to leave one copy of the apparatus behind is for one of the gametes to leave everything but the nucleus behind, including the mitochondria.

We are thus led to the model that Mother Nature discovered the male gamete as a vehicle to promote the fusion of nuclei. Two haploid nuclei, each sitting in its own mitotic apparatus in a common cytoplasm, need not fuse to survive and proliferate and, indeed, may have logistical difficulties getting together. On the other hand, if one of the nuclei lacks a mitotic apparatus, its success will require access to that of the other nucleus, and it achieves this access by becoming one with the other. If we insist upon using emotion laden words to describe this arrangement, *sharing* is vastly superior to *selfish*.[22]

The role of the egg in development is so dramatic and central that we tend to pay minimal attention to the role of the sperm, as if it were little more than a spark that starts a conflagration—the transitory role of the spark is acknowledged, but one is inclined to watch the fire. When the diminutive sperm unites with an egg, it does provide one of the key signals in the chain of developmental events—a kind of spark. The outline of what the sperm does in this process is well established. It fuses with the egg membrane by a very elaborate mechanism, its nucleus migrates to the egg nucleus, and the two nuclei then fuse. We almost never pay attention to what the sperm doesn't do. It doesn't disrupt the egg's gradients of morphogens.

174

For contrast, imagine a fertilization process in which an egg gets fertilized by another egg. One supposes that morphogenetic pandemonium would ensue. It is one matter to picture a single nucleus, by slipping through the morphogenetic fields of the egg cytoplasm, causing no disruption, and another matter altogether to mix two full complements of cytoplasm. The point of this little thought experiment is that the invention of the nucleus-only gamete, which only later became associated with the male sexual function, may be necessary for more than the preservation of morphogenetic fields. It may also have been a precondition for the very invention of the gradients of the egg—and, therefore, a precondition to the Cambrian explosion. Perhaps only by having a fertilization mechanism that allows the contribution from one parent a stealthy entry, in effect, could the experiments in morphogenetic gradients have been undertaken within the larger gamete contributed by the second parent. If this is the case, the Cambrian explosion is the culmination of a series of inventions, each possible only in the aftermath of the one before. The ordered series includes cell fusion, meiosis, the diminutive sperm and the morphogenetic egg.

If the diminutive gamete had its beginnings as an innovation in the process of bringing haploid nuclei together for fusion, organisms without dimorphic gametes may have discovered a different mechanism. Since the latter organisms cannot produce eggs, they have remained very simple in design. The possibility clearly exists that different strategies of uniting haploid nuclei have played pivotal historical roles in the divergence of unicellular and multicellular lineages. It would seem well worth our while to learn the mechanisms by which nuclei are transported through cytoplasm in these two types of system.

Of one thing we can be confident. Mechanisms that transport nuclei are solutions to the logistical problems of genes, not expressions of selfishness. It has become increasingly difficult to understand the continuing appeal of an idea so uniformly tiresome and misleading as the idea that genes are selfish. Every existing gene represents the discovery of a truthful recognition of the world within which that gene functions. Every existing gene and, thus, every existing genetic statement of truth has survived all previous challenges to its validity. As we turn our attention to the aftermath of the Cambrian explosion, we will do so in the spirit of truth telling, eschewing all thoughts of selfishness. Everything that follows is in the spirit and celebration of truthful recognition.

7. Is Anything Out There Looking at You?

Suppose you are looking at your pet across the room or yourself in the mirror. In either case, what you are seeing is one cell reiterated many times—in your case about 100 trillion times. Each of those many cells is a direct, genetically identical descendant of one cell (the zygote). However, each of those genetically identical cells has interpreted its place in the collection of cells that comprise the whole organism and then, chameleon-like, has adopted one of the guises in its repertory. The human cell has a repertory of about 200 guises—representing the 200 different types of cells in the human organism. Each of these cell types differs from all others by the combination of genes that are, or have been active within it.

To someone unaccustomed to thinking about biological systems, it may seem a harsh critique to define an individual as a massive reiteration but, as we have seen, the harshness doesn't end there—the individual reiteration is also a biological dead-end. The universal biological property of multicellular senescence assures that multicellular reiterations will cease to exist. A reiteration can leave a biological legacy only if it reproduces. In a supreme irony, it must also then cease to exist. Darwinian biology is predicated on a system in which subsequent generations replace prior generations—each generation is ultimately obligated to make room for its descendants.

Since the multicellular individual—the reiteration of a single cell—ceases to exist unless it reproduces, and must then cease to exist anyway, it is one of Nature's finer paradoxes that the multicellular individual also reproduces by the very act of ceasing to exist. That is, the multicellular individual reverts to the most primitive of all conditions—a haploid single cell—in order to resurrect itself (with the now standard caveat that it resurrects an approximation of itself). It is a little as if the rites of sexual reproduction require a kind of homage to our most ancient ancestors–the haploid single cells that invented sex, and therefore us, in the first place. It may not be metaphysically pleasing, but it is logically inescapable that the germ line produced us and not the other way around.

But even as we marvel at the central role of single cells, the rest of our narrative must focus on the biological properties of multicellular systems. Before doing so, it will be useful to outline the major accomplishments of the single cell.

1. The single cell, during the first billion or so years of its existence, became a master chemist.
2. Through cell fusion, the single cell discovered the diploid condition (from which it had a built-in meiotic escape).
3. The single cell was able to exploit the diploidy-escape system to begin a new exploration of its environment with diploid, multicellular forms.

Each generation, the single cell escaped the multicellular condition *via* meiosis and produced new, variant individuals of a subsequent generation who could thus explore the environment anew and then, in their own time, escape to form yet another succeeding generation.

4. The single cell was able, secondarily, to exploit the diploidy-escape system to invent development—that is, the egg and its bipartite genetic systems.

At the heart of this series of inventions is the chemical wizardry of the single cell. Single cells ultimately became such accomplished chemists that they could vary their chemistry according to the circumstances in which they found themselves. As we have seen, genetically identical cells can express themselves in hundreds of different ways. During development from the single cell of a human zygote, for example, each of the hundred trillion cells of the adult comes to possess its particular chemical properties, and thus biological properties, as a function of its developmental experience. Identical cells behave non-identically as a consequence of serial responses to their immediate environments. We will refer to this capacity to the same cell to be many different things as the contingency principle. We will later return to the contingency principle in a surprising way.

Once we have recognized and acknowledged that an individual metazoan, like a fruit fly or a human, is a single, reiterated cell and, as a participant in life's continuity, is the germ line's way of making more (approximations) of itself, we might also seem to have trivialized the importance of multicellular existence. We will develop instead the more sanguine view that by describing our existence in such humble terms, which are nonetheless faithful to the facts, we have positioned ourselves to see that the truth is more astonishing than we would have imagined. Far from trivializing multicellular life, this humble view of the lives of individuals allows us to focus more clearly and confidently on questions that usually seem beyond the pale of science. In particular, we can ask whether single cells achieved some sort of dramatic breakthrough in their capacity to recognize their surroundings. Did single cells discover anything we might call transcendental while making the transition to a multicellular life style? We will answer this question in the affirmative and, in doing so, will violate no laws of chemistry or physics. There is no magic—just layers of recognition coming increasingly closer to the truth.

We have already touched upon one outgrowth of being multicellular—that of doing two or more things simultaneously. We used the example of feeding and swimming as alternative states of existence in the single-celled organism *Naegleria*, but as cohabiting states in multicellular descendants of such single-celled ancestors. However, the coordinate expression of pre-existing properties falls short of a transcendent achievement. We are in search of an emergent property—something that completely eludes single cell life styles.

One type of emergent property achieved by groups of cells is that of extracellular digestion. Through the creation of a lumen or gut, multicellular forms evolved the capacity to utilize a broader range of types and sizes of nutrients—especially other multicellular organisms or their by-products. Among other things, this allows the feeder to eat and run. The idea of extracellular digestion is not entirely unique to multicellular life, however, inasmuch as single fungal and bacterial cells also make some use of the technique. They, of course, must settle into the medium they are consuming, instead of ingesting it whole, and certainly cannot eat and run. They must sit and eat.

A second type of emergent property is found in the kinetic mechanisms of multicellular organisms— no unicellular organism can contract itself in quite the same way as a muscle cell and no unicell produces bones and ligaments to generate self-contained leverage. Once again, however, even in the realm of kinesis, we have to take note of analogous functions in single cells. In fact, many of the macromolecules used in multicellular kinetic activities—muscle proteins like actin and myosin, for example—are also found in single-celled organisms where they play roles in kinetic activities like amoeboid and flagellar motion. In other words, multicellular kinetics can be portrayed as evolutionary extensions of single cell ideas. The lever, like the gut, is crucial to the success of multicellular organisms, but fails to inspire thoughts of transcendence.

Although advances in digestion and locomotion are impressive in their own right, the transcendental jackpot we are looking for is, of course, right where we would have expected to find it all along—in those extraordinary animal information systems we call the senses and the neuronal network that ties them together. While this may seem so self-evident that its mention is anticlimactic, we can sometimes surprise ourselves by looking again at well known things, especially if we look at them in slightly different ways. The topic we will examine in a new light is not just the senses but the whole of biological recognition and what it means to recognize.

You will recall that our single-celled ancestors spent some three billion years advancing the cause of recognition and setting the stage for multicellular life. The bedrock of their invention is the collection of forms and functions described by the central dogma. The interactions of DNA, RNA and proteins are precisely and without exception based on recognition at the molecular level. In other words, the biological capacity to transmit biological information is predicated squarely on rules of chemical recognition.

182

Multicellular life is, in turn, built up from single cells through innovations in chemical recognition. All cell-cell recognition and adhesion is based upon the chemistry of molecules recognizing each other.

In the course of our review of these molecular and cellular hierarchies of recognition, we have also begun to flirt with the idea that increasingly sophisticated recognition can achieve a status more aptly defined as interpretation. For example, in biosynthesis, a molecule is recognized or interpreted as a subunit that can be used in the construction of a needed product. At the level of cell-cell interaction, a given cell in a given place recognizes or interprets its neighbors and responds by adjusting its genetic expression.

The relatively recent inventions of multicellular senses—especially vision, hearing and touch—represent nothing less than a quantum leap in the capacity to recognize and interpret the environment. The basis of the leap is a fundamental reordering of the criteria utilized in recognition. The single cell, as we have seen, assesses its environment through the receipt and analysis of essentially chemical signals. Multicellular sensory systems added on top of the single cell's chemical repertory the capacity to receive and analyze physical signals. At the Cambrian explosion, the unicellular organisms, already astonishingly adept chemists, began to reinvent themselves as physicists. In other words, unicellular organisms which had inherited a largely chemical interpretation of their world, began evolving and transmitting to subsequent generations a physical interpretation as well.

Powerful selective advantages have accrued to organisms with senses that monitor the physical environment. Indeed, from our modern perspective, the advantages are so obvious that they tend to obscure the considerable problems that came along as baggage. While the pre-Cambrian cells played by one set of rules (almost entirely chemical), their post-Cambrian descendants had to begin learning another, equally or more difficult, set of physical rules. The new rules are so difficult, in fact, that 500 million years after the Cambrian explosion we are still struggling to master them.

Consider this. The pre-Cambrian single cell chemists were confined to life styles that utilized mainly qualitative, yes-or-no, on-or-off kinds of environmental interpretation. They invented these interpretations in the face of such questions as whether or not to engulf what they bump into, whether to swim or sit still and whether it's time to divide. It is fair to say that each time a unicellular organism commits an act of interpretation, it elicits an all or none response.

In contrast, when multicellular organisms began experimenting with mechanisms that gathered and assessed physical information, represented as

184

light and sound and pressure, they began to take account of other objects, including other organisms, at a distance from themselves. Their encounters with those objects were no longer governed so much by chance but became increasingly the consequence of explicit action. They began to evolve the capacity to give chase and take flight. Over time, the survivors in this world of new rules developed the capacity to assess relative properties of distant objects, such as size, speed and even intentions. In a word, the new multicellular physicists invented the art of estimation. In this new world, yes-or-no responses continued to guide the activities of individual cells, but probabilistic responses were invented to help guide the collective or coordinate activities of whole multicellular organisms. Perhaps we can think of that period in biological history in terms of a great burst of language acquisition: the yes-no vocabulary gradually became enriched by big-small, fast-slow, approaching-departing, predator-prey and, at some point, one of the more poignant questions—is that thing one of my own?

However, in a least one very important sense, not much changed at the Cambrian explosion. The pre-Cambrian single-celled chemists and their more highly educated multicellular descendants both had to cope with exactly the same core problems. They had to nourish themselves and, succeeding at that, they had to reproduce. One of the few things we know with certainty about all ancestors is that they succeeded in these two endeavors.

Success in solving the nourishment problem is, to be precise, success in the act of acquiring subunits, either by manufacturing them (as a tree does) or by obtaining them from another organism (as a lion does). But trees manufacture their subunits with processes like photosynthesis, invented by their pre-Cambrian single-celled ancestors. Similarly, predation is a very old game. The early unicellular predators were every bit as unsympathetic as any modern predator. In that they engulfed their prey whole, they were the equivalent of snakes in the pre-Cambrian seas.

Modern predation, as practiced by multicellular organisms, is certainly more elaborate than the predatory methods of single cells but achieves exactly the same end. Whether we are talking about a shark, a cobra or a cheetah, every predator is a subunit borrower who ultimately repays the loan—usually through middlemen like bacteria, fly larvae, vultures and other scavengers. Whether we are talking about a guppy, a rat or a gazelle, every target of predation is a subunit bank that ultimately loans all assets, either directly or through the scavenger back-up system. Mother Nature discovered recycling long ago and remains fastidious and ardent on the subject.

The advent of the multicellular life style had an impact on reproduction similar to that on predation—

186

the outcome of reproduction changed little while the means to achieve it became highly elaborate and even ritualized. This view, of course, is based upon the interpretation that the germ line is the means for reproductive continuity, rather than its product. Even though we humans are determined to take pride in our humanity, as if the means of nourishing and reproducing our cell were on a higher plane—the available evidence is less than compelling that we systematically undertake these activities in any especially analytical way.

Could it be, then, that not much really changed at the Cambrian explosion—that multicellular organisms are a sort of biological better mouse trap? Or can we ferret out a meaning from these new mouse traps that is more than better cuisine and better sex? We will look for the answer not so much in the better mouse traps themselves, but in the nature of the problems that were resolved *en route* to producing those better mouse traps. The secret may be in the questions.

We can be thoroughly confident that the early systems for taking physical measurements of the environment were crude and that advances in the sensitivities and coordination of these systems introduced new standards of ambiguity. Indeed, the early stages in the emergence of cells as physicists may mark the very invention of ambiguity. Although it is rather difficult to empathize with the way simpler organisms perceive their environments, we know certainly in ourselves and other mammals, as well as birds and reptiles, that there are constant challenges that arise in ways that strain the capacity of the senses. Consider the following sorts of practical questions:

- Is that a stick you see in front of you—or is that a snake?
- Is that the wind you hear in the bushes—or is that something that would like to borrow your subunits?
- Is there anything out there looking at you?

Given that ambiguity is present, there is powerful selection in favor of innovations that resolve ambiguity. Given that a truth can be shrouded in ambiguity, getting at that truth requires tackling ambiguity itself. It is in ambiguity, then, that we will search for the meaning of life. First, however, we must negotiate the minefield of hallucination. Please notice that we have wandered into an area ripe for charlatanism and other forms of nonsense. We might as well have some fun with it.

8. Rats, Cats and Snakes

In one of the more idyllic periods of my childhood, my family lived on 200 acres of prime farmland in the northeast of Washington State. Although the winters in the area could be harsh, the remainder of the year was remarkably mild. We enjoyed long warm days, rich soil and riparian rights in the Kettle River—the locals were fond of saying that a person could make a living there by accident. However, markets were distant, so it was difficult to achieve much more than a living and put anything aside. For that reason, among others, we eventually moved away.

One especially fine fall day during my sixth year, my mother and father and I were walking across a fallow field that stretched off to the south from the barnyard towards a stand of second growth Ponderosa pines and Douglas firs. Among the pines and firs lay a series of small spring-fed ponds. Although none of us any longer remembers the reason for our walk that day, we do remember being accompanied by the Holstein we called Molly. Molly was something of a pet and seemed to enjoy our company as we did hers. She was also highly prized for her apparent willingness to provide a major part of our domestic milk supply.

It was Molly's habit during these walks to keep a bit in front of us, stopping now and then to graze upon whatever might happen to be available. Given the dry conditions of the fall season, most of the volunteer grasses growing there had long since been toppled and provided more of a carpet underfoot than anything to eat. The walking was easy and with the constant drone of countless grasshoppers one could lapse into a frame of mind that was sometimes hard to tell from sleep. Each time we caught up to Molly, she would hurry ahead a short distance and stop again to pick at the foliage.

As we approached her during one of these cycles, a small garter snake darted from just inches beyond her nose and raced away. Molly let out a mighty grunt as she leapt straight backwards. Although she reacted with great urgency and effort, her leap probably covered little more than a foot of ground. Since none of us was directly behind her, we allowed ourselves a good chuckle at Molly's expense. You would have to observe a grunting and jumping cow to appreciate fully what an unwieldy contrivance that is.

While the story of Molly and the snake has survived for years as a piece of family lore, it also evolved into a series of questions. Why would a very large cow be induced to jump, violently as it happened, by the mere movement of a tiny snake? How was it that Molly didn't see the snake until it moved, but when it did move she acted as though she knew what it was? Since there was never reason to think that Molly had any prior training in snakes, what predilection could she possibly have had about the sudden motion in the stubble of that field?

190

Years later, there occurred a variation on the theme of pets and snakes when a friend and I were driving through California's Central Valley. We were accompanied not by a cow, but by our two magnificent Samoyed dogs. (Marsha, whom you will meet again later, considered them to be her magnificent Samoyeds. Incidentally, that seems to be pronounced sam'-e-yed as opposed to sa-moy'-ed or the incomprehensible but commonly heard sa-moy'-an).

At a rest stop, I took the dogs on leashes to an area set aside for pets to do their version of resting. California is a place of great thoughtfulness, no matter what foreigners may think. When I removed the leashes, the dogs went ahead of me onto the expanse of lawn, their noses to the ground. Characteristically, they pursued their exploration side-by-side, their flanks touching in such a way that they seemed to lean into each other.

After about twenty of my paces—the dogs were probably fifteen feet ahead of me—I froze in my tracks. They had come upon and then stepped right over a snake lying at a right angle to their path. The snake was quite a husky fellow, maybe four feet long, cream colored with pink or perhaps salmon highlights along is sides. I still don't know what kind of snake it was. It remained motionless as eight magnificent Samoyed feet neatly avoided stepping on it, much as they might avoid stepping on a stick. As soon as they had accomplished this traverse, I hurried around behind the snake, called the dogs and reattached their leashes. Thinking I was in control, I turned back to get a better look. The snake had, by whatever means in whatever direction, disappeared from sight.

Unlike the Molly episode, this one did not at first seem humorous––my unfamiliarity with that kind of snake and my initial fear for the safety of the dogs had given me a jolting dose of adrenaline. On the other hand, like the Molly episode, this, too, evolved into a question. How was it that the dogs, who apparently saw something to avoid stepping on, nonetheless failed to see a snake easily visible to a human fifteen feet away? As it turns out, the relationships of dogs and cows to snakes strains to tell us something.

We have been developing the thesis that life is built upon recognition. In its most dramatic form, the thesis is that recognition is the organizing principle of life. From the very origin of life, and continuing for some three billion years of evolution, recognition was almost exclusively a chemical phenomenon. During those three billion years, single cells became master chemists. They even became masters of chemical contingency, counteracting and even exploiting chemical changes in their environments with chemical changes of their own.

We have outlined the rationale that the advent of multicellular life, itself a chemistry-based

192

phenomenon, set the stage for the invention of the senses, those biological instruments that specialize in the collection of physical information from the environment. In keeping with the thesis that life follows recognition, the selective advantages attached to the senses follow exactly from the increased capacity to recognize one's surroundings; we animals use our senses of sight, hearing, touch, smell and even taste to recognize and interpret where we are and what is going on there. When we say that a particular animal is adapted to a particular niche, we could as well be saying that it is good at recognizing and interpreting that niche.

Whether we say "adapted to a niche" or "good at recognizing and interpreting a niche," there will be a premium on improving the accuracy of the adaptation or recognition. Much of the text that follows is an informal examination of the nature of recognition at the pinnacle of its power and accuracy--within mammalian nervous systems. The focus of this examination will be on the kinds of problems that have had to be solved and the process of solving them. A review of state-of-the-art neurobiology is willingly left to experts in the field.

However, even lacking expertise, we can't help but notice that the fundamental organization of nervous systems is ancient and conservative. The organisms of the Burgess Shale, more than 500 million years old, already possessed an organization at least analogous and probably homologous to modern insects. A fruit fly, as an example of the latter group, has sensory nerves that participate in the collection of physical data from the environment, motor nerves that participate in the control of mechanical activity and a central ganglion—a rudimentary brain located in the region of the head—that acts in the coordination and integration of these functions. This basic design is found also in fishes, reptiles, birds and mammals. It was probably invented once. The profundity of elaborations on the prototype is too obvious to require any comment here.

The task of any nervous system is to make sense of inputs and to fashion useful outputs. A beam of light falling on an eye has no intrinsic meaning to the eye but can have meaning to the owner of the eye if the physical properties of the light can be translated into some form of biological information. One must make sense of the light. The owner of the eye may want to run away from the light if the nervous system attached to the eye discerns that the light just bounced off *Tyrannosaurus rex*, for example. The role of the eye in this chain of events is to collect raw physical data. The nervous system converts the physical data to biological data. Clearly, the conversion of physical data to biological data can be a most useful thing, especially if it is accurate. It is worth knowing if *T. rex* is closing ground or moving away. The conversion is most likely to be useful if it tells the truth. It is particularly useful if the system also knows what the truth means or portends. Designing and building a

194

truthful conversion system is thus an enterprise predicated on a straightforward logic—if you cannot see and tell the truth, you may not be a candidate for survival.

There is, of course, a small problem in designing and building a conversion system. Neither the conversion system itself nor Natural Selection starts out on this project knowing what the truth is (Natural Selection would be very content to mistake coming for going if that mistake conferred selective advantage). This means that designing and building the conversion system must be conducted as a series of experiments under the same constraints that apply to all biological experiments. The design phase is the random, accidental occurrence of mutations. The testing phase is the scrutiny of the design's worth by Natural Selection. The conversion instrument is put together piecemeal. Given the experimental nature of building a nervous system, we can be sure that early versions were imprecise and that Natural Selection favoring improvements would have been intense.

The evolving system would have been plagued with at least two major categories of problem. On the one hand, the system originated in a state of complete ignorance. Everything new had to be ambiguous. Secondly, for every function that evolution added to the system, there had to follow a means of controlling that function. An initial lack of control, whether by way of misconnection or misfiring, would generate hallucination. Ambiguity and hallucination are intrinsic to the nervous system and remain important characteristics even today. They were surely issues in every stage of nervous system evolution.

One of the ways we might gain insight into the nature of changes in nervous systems across time is through comparative studies of existing species. The rationale of such an approach is that the brains of a variety of animal types represent vignettes of evolutionary time. To a first approximation, the brain of a snake is a one- or two-hundred-million-year-old reptilian structure, while that of a human is a derivative brain perhaps as little as 100,000 years old (this is not to say that they are representatives of a linear array of brains). If we knew everything about these two types of brain, and about those of intermediate complexity, we would have very educated ideas about how Mother Nature got from one to another.

Unfortunately, we do not at present know everything about any nervous system, let alone all systems, and my own familiarity with the knowledge that does exist is modest. This leaves me to share some comparative observations over which I have been puzzling for nearly two decades. Fortunately, these observations lead to some testable, if slightly fanciful, predictions about the organizing principles of vertebrate perceptions of their universe.

The first subject of these observations was a snake–a boa constrictor about six feet in length. She

196

carried the name Bubbles on account of a fungal infection with which she had been afflicted as a young snake that had caused her to froth at the mouth. Bubbles was the pet snake of my housemate. They had been separated for several years and their reunion constituted for me an abrupt introduction, not just to Bubbles, but to the whole notion of a snake as a pet. I had had numerous encounters with snakes in the wild and was never especially squeamish about them, but this was new ground. Bubbles was the first snake I could watch at will, even if the conditions were less than natural. I was to become amazed.

For the first couple of weeks after our introduction, Bubbles lay coiled in her terrarium, a roomy box with a glass front and top. She would stay apparently motionless for hours on end as if inanimate, although her eyes were exceedingly bright. With just a little patience, it was possible to discern the motion of her breathing. From time to time she would be at her water bowl and then back to her timeless coil.

One morning the coil had transformed itself into a very active snake and my education began in earnest. Bubbles was crawling here and there and stretching to examine every seam and corner of the terrarium. Her tongue had begun the incessant flicking we take as the virtual signature of a snake.

After I'd been watching this commotion awhile, Marsha also noticed it and came to join me.

"Look who's hungry," she said. "I'll bring a rat from work tonight."

I should have guessed that the activity signaled hunger but had not. I also should have guessed dinner would be a rat but was momentarily surprised upon hearing it. In fact, I had never thought about the logistics of a snake as pet. I suppose that all of us have become inclined to think of domestic animals eating what we give them, usually out of a can or a box. But neither vegetables nor by-products of a slaughterhouse will do for a constrictor. They recognize things like intact, preferably live rodents for food. There are snakes with other specialties, of course, such as those that recognize and take eggs and even those that take other snakes, but Bubbles was a rodent-recognizing specialist. In at least the realm of diet, one is unlikely to tame a snake.

That evening, Marsha produced the promised rat (from the colony of laboratory rats maintained by the research group in which she worked) and put it in Bubbles' terrarium. I admit to having felt a bit of revulsion, but my vague impulse to rescue the rat lacked any real motive power. I simply had not developed any empathy for rats (one would guess that a person with a pet rat would avoid a pet snake, and vice versa). To the extent that the level of empathy was low, however, the level of fascination was high and easily suppressed the revulsion; I was bound to watch. As it turns out, the process by which a constrictor kills and eats a rat is less grisly than I

198

had expected. For one thing, it happens so quickly that the details are hard to see.

When the rat was placed in the terrarium, Bubbles quickly ceased her searching activity. Then, keeping a constant vigilance––she was looking directly at the rat and still sampling the air from time to time with her signature tongue––she began forming herself into a coil. In much the same way that one would have to see a cow jump to appreciate that form of awkwardness, one would surely have to observe a constrictor make preparation for a strike to fully appreciate the deliberateness and patience (and grace) with which that behavior unfolds. Bubbles' movement was barely perceptible, particularly when the rat was looking her way. At various points during this period of preparation, for example when the rat stopped to scratch himself and had his snout pointed elsewhere, Bubbles would dramatically quicken the pace of her coiling, but return to the deliberate mode when the rat's distraction ended. Soon after she had begun her coiling, she also stopped sampling the air. Presumably, the sight of the rat had eliminated any need for confirmation by smell.

Meanwhile, the rat had begun to explore the terrarium. He approached and examined the water bowl, walked past it on the back side and then walked up and onto the most prominent feature of the terrarium's interior. The rat was standing on Bubbles. My mouth was probably open, but Bubbles seemed oddly unperturbed by this turn of events. She doubled back on herself and was thus still able to watch the rat. I was cursing myself for not having a camera on hand.

That particular rat might have been written off as a buffoon among rats, but I gradually became convinced that his behavior revealed a simple truth about his species. Rats are about as able to see snakes as are cows and dogs. The rat in question recognized and negotiated Bubbles as a topological feature of the environment, but was unable to recognize Bubbles for what she was. Bubbles was a hungry snake moments from dinner.

In any event, the rat walked down from Bubbles in the direction from which he had come. My impression was that he had begun to sense that something was wrong. Perhaps a rat standing on a snake notices that the footing is peculiar and that had gotten his attention. Perhaps he had detected an odor of snake. About two feet away from Bubbles he turned back towards her and was sniffing the air (I would describe it as sniffing hard in Bubbles' direction if such an act is possible). It turns out that the worst mistake a rat can make is to look at a hungry constrictor. That rat face, pointed straight at her, was apparently just the target she wanted.

Bubbles struck, the rat leapt straight into the air, Bubbles' head passed directly beneath him, she recoiled and he returned to earth. They were back in their starting positions. It is only the mildest

200

hyperbole to say that if I had blinked, I would have missed it.

It is necessary here for me to make a little confession that serves to place the rat's leap in a larger context. My confession is about cats—animals that I really like and enjoy—but there is a certain torment of cats I am unable to resist. The ideal form of this torment is a rope lying on the ground, one end in the tormentor's hand, and a cat nearby. The cat approaches the rope, perhaps looking at it or perhaps not, and when the cat arrives at the rope, the tormentor gives it a little tug. The cat almost invariably leaps straight into the air. One of my cats could do a documented six feet. Another would sometimes turn a somersault before returning to the ground.

I would not confess this terrible secret, but the vaulting behavior of cats always perplexed me as much as it amazed me—until, that is, I saw the rat avoid Bubbles. Rats, like cats, seem to be wired to leap into the air in response to a sudden movement on the horizontal. Such a leap is a reasonably effective solution to the problem of a striking snake. A sudden movement on the horizontal may mean *snake* in the rat and cat view of the world—not to mention Holsteins who can only effect a small leap backwards.

Meanwhile, the hapless rat trapped in Bubbles' terrarium had no decent options upon his own return to ground level. I would have expected him to run to a corner or behind the water bowl, but he essentially crouched where he had landed and continued to look in the direction of Bubbles, who, the second time, was right on target.

The train of events in a successful strike can only be told in slow motion. In truth, what I can provide is an impression and interpretation of a strike. In the first place, based on the few times I've seen it, the strike of a snake is one of Mother Nature's premier demonstrations of quickness. For a constrictor, it goes something like this: The snake must first position itself within a distance on the order of a third of its body length from its intended victim. It is able to do this because its intended victim—such as a rat—cannot recognize snakes. It strikes at its victims' face, a technique that has at least two salutary effects for the snake. Once it has closed its mouth around that of its victim, the victim is not only prevented from biting the snake, but also has its breathing impaired or blocked. The snake then coils itself around the victim's torso and begins the powerful constrictions that effectively paralyze the victim's diaphragm. In Bubble's case, the coils were thrown around the victim and the constrictions were applied at the approximate location from which she had initiated the strike. That is, she essentially snatched the rat from where it had been and brought it back to the place she had been, effecting the coils in the process. With the coils in place, one might see nothing of the rat but its tail and sometimes not that.

202

It is put very much under wraps (The details of snatching and obscuring the rat play a key role in a later part of our story). Then, with the rat's mouth covered, she would constrict its breathing apparatus until it died of suffocation. I've seen Bubbles prepare a rat for consumption in about a minute.

At some signal, which I would guess to be the end of convulsions, Bubbles would uncoil from the rat and release it, take the rat, still face first, back into her mouth and swallow it whole. For the following couple of days, it would be possible to monitor the rat's fate in the form of a bulge being transported along Bubbles' long torso (if you have read *The Little Prince* you will immediately recognize the phenomenon). The bulge would gradually disappear as the rat's components were dissociated into their subunits, destined for reassembly as snake components. We said earlier that Bubbles was a rat-recognizing specialist. Once she recognized a rat, she proceeded to recycle it.

I came away from my first experience with Bubbles' ideas about nutrition thinking I had learned three things.

- An outline of her feeding technique.
- That rats cannot recognize snakes.
- That rats carry a congenital message:
    (a) *Sudden motion equals snake.*
    (b) *Jump.*

Whether I had my lessons straight, Bubbles was clearly a provocative teacher. However, the next time I saw her feed, her effectiveness was heightened by the presence of two teaching assistants. The two assistants were cats and, together with Bubbles, they showed me things that are difficult to see. The diverse personalities of these cats were critical to their effectiveness, so I must describe them in some detail.

KihEe. Our home in Palo Alto was in a tract built shortly after World War II. Like nearly all of the homes in the neighborhood, it had a driveway leading past the house to a small, detached garage towards the rear of the lot. Our garage had a full-length canopied storage area facing the large and fenced backyard. We used this covered space to store a winter's supply of firewood. At the rear of the canopy, away from the house, I had set aside an area for chopping and splitting wood. By the end of the first winter, a thick bed of chips and bark had accumulated. I first met KihEe when he came to this spot to convalesce or, perhaps, to die.

His choice of sites was a sensible one. Many of the households in the neighborhood, on both sides of the rear fence, tended not to make much use of the part of their lots behind the line described by the rear walls of the garages. Consequently, there was a grove of trees co-extensive across about twenty lots and covering nearly an acre of ground. Our lot was at one end of this insular forest.

Anyone passing through the neighborhood could see a green-belt and probably feel some of the resulting serenity, including constant bird song and chatter. But for someone in a position to observe a little more closely, it also emerged as home to a little colony of feral cats.

One member of the colony, who would explore our yard from time to time, was a magnificent tomcat with Siamese markings. I always spoke to him but was never allowed nearer than thirty or forty feet before he would slip back into his sanctuary. Even when jumping the six-foot fence, his movements asserted that life was effortless and high fences could be scaled without a sound. Everything looked easy. He was some cat.

Returning home one evening, I entered the backyard through the gate in the fence connecting the house and garage. From there, I began to wander through our lush and productive vegetable garden. The soil in Palo Alto is a gardener's delight. I had gotten to within about twenty feet of the rear of the woodpile when I saw the movement of the big Siamese fellow getting up from his resting place in the chips and bark. As he disappeared behind the garage, I spoke to him as usual and hoped that this encounter meant he shared my interest in becoming acquainted.

The following evening he was there again. I was allowed to approach even closer but now could see that his tolerance of my presence was not voluntary. He watched me come to within eight or ten feet, struggled to his feet and moved away. His usual grace was gone. In fact, his movements were labored and he even staggered. I could probably have caught him and picked him up but was, frankly, afraid to touch him. He went under the fence in the direction of the little forest.

I went to check the woodpile the next dawn. He had come back in the night and now made no apparent effort to move away from me. He reeked of urine. I retrieved a heavy cardboard box from the garage and, its top open, inverted it over him. By slowly sliding a scrap of plywood under the box, and therefore also under the cat, it was possible to completely entrap him. Finally, I carefully tipped box and plywood until the open end of the box faced up and peeked inside. The cat was at the bottom and had righted himself but made no other movement. I closed the top of the box and secured it.

Marsha volunteered for the next step, which was to drive the boxed cat to a veterinarian--we thought to be euthanized. What followed instead was a celebration of competence. The vet looked into the box, reached in and picked up the cat, placed him on the examining table and announced the diagnosis (I only remember that it was viral). He would keep him under observation for a couple of days and treat him for dehydration and the bacterial infection of the ulcers on the cat's face (I suppose these ulcers were important to the vet's quick diagnosis). In short, with a little water and some antibiotics, the cat would survive. Marsha, with typical presence of mind, asked that the vet also relieve the cat of his particular variety of hormone poisoning.

Three days later, the big cat was put back in the box and discharged from the vet's. After driving home, we carried the box into a spare room, opened it, and out flew the cat. He went immediately behind an old television cabinet—one of the early types with doors that closed over the front of the set. The electronics had long since been removed from the set and junked, so the cat found himself in an enclosed space with ample room to stretch (the cabinet had been given to us by a neighbor so that we could salvage the cherrywood from which it was built—as unbelievable as cherrywood television cabinets might seem these days). We did not open the cabinet doors but conspired to coax him out. We had the food, after all, and he was sure to get hungry. We saw nothing more of him that first day.

Upon returning from work the following day, I went straight into the house rather than the garden. It was clear that he had been out of his cabinet to visit both the litter box and the water bowl. I put a small dish of surprisingly aromatic cat food on the floor about two feet from the cabinet and then sat on the floor next to the plate on the side opposite the cabinet. He soon appeared but crouched and watched me from the space between cabinet and wall. After about ten minutes of this stand-off, I pushed the plate next to the cabinet and went outside. He ate.

We repeated this routine just once. The next day he came out from the cabinet, approached the food cautiously and began to eat. When he was about half finished, he allowed me to stroke his head. He had moved in.

There are two brief stories about KihEe that will round out our review of his character. The first of these is based on an event that occurred when he was given the run of the house after a few days of convalescence in the closed room. He at first eyed the dogs warily—the same dogs that had earlier stepped over the snake—and they him, as everyone kept a discreet distance. The first night of his new freedom, he came right into the bedroom, crawled under the covers and stretched out next to me. I was thinking that I certainly had a cat and he was probably thinking just the opposite.

This arrangement precipitated a near disaster the next morning. It was the dogs' habit to come to bedside at first light and agitate to be let outdoors. When they began poking me with their gorgeous snouts, KihEe burst from under the covers and caught the male with a ferocious swat about midway between the tip of his nose and his eyes. Four little beads of blood appeared as the dogs backed off. Peace ultimately prevailed and within no more than a month KihEe ate with the dogs, slept with the dogs (an arrangement we preferred), exchanged grooming with the dogs and even engaged in a game of tag they

208

invented in the backyard. To my knowledge, KihEe never again strayed beyond our fences.

The second story about KihEe dovetails with Siamese cat lore and gave us a scare much worse than that from the battery on the dogs. One of our nearest neighbors often came to visit, her toddler in tow. On occasion, she would leave him with us while she returned home to look after some chore or other. Her little boy liked this arrangement, especially when we were in the backyard because of the novel things to examine there, like a woodpile, a garden and all those animals–each of whom was solicitous of children. He didn't know about Bubbles.

On one of these occasions, the boy's grandmother came in place of his mother to escort him home. It was her first and last visit to our yard. She came about ten feet inside the gate and called the boy, rather brusquely, who was across the yard from her, helping Marsha harvest tomatoes. I was farther back in the yard and looked up to greet Grandma. Before I could say a word, KihEe, from somewhere behind me, went past at a dead sprint, positioned himself in a menacing crouch squarely between the child and his grandmother and—with ears laid flat against his head—produced a sickening sound that was some combination of scream and growl. Grandma wisely turned and headed for the gate. The little boy smiled broadly at this development. Marsha and I stood and trembled. A few moments later, the boy's mother came to get him and did so without incident. It is an indelible memory that KihEe watched the latter episode as he sat and washed his face. Momma he knew, but it seemed that no stranger would touch that child on his watch.

KihEe was heroic. He was loyal, robust, affectionate and silly. I don't recall exactly when or how he got tagged with his name, but it seemed to describe what he was so it stuck. He was about to become my teacher.

TeeDee. We had come to Palo Alto from Seattle, a city with a number of compelling features. A travel brochure would brag about the beautiful mountains, Puget Sound and the Pike Street Market, for example. The brochure would contain little mention of the likelihood of rain. Perhaps on account of the rain, around the streets of Seattle you will also see some of the worlds' most beautiful cats, as if only the hale and hearty survive. However, as we know well, there are always exceptions and our little apartment in the University District was next door to one. The kindly lady who lived there had a black and white, long-haired female cat that resembled a certain cartoon character on the one hand, and was at most phlegmatic on the other. She rarely appeared to be doing anything.

Then, to our amazement, one night she came into our apartment through an open window and produced a litter of three kittens, in a tip-out bin among our kitchen cabinets that was probably

210

designed to hold grain or flour but which we used for bread. It had been left empty and open that night.

When we first discovered mother and her brood, one of the kittens—a pure white male—was dead. For various reasons, we guessed him to have been stillborn. The other two kittens were both females with essentially all black coats. One looked like a proverbial ugly duckling and grew up to be an ugly cat. She was scrawny and bug-eyed, but her sorry demeanor hid a clever and athletic cat. If scales of intelligence were meaningful, and something we monitored and labeled in cats, she would surely have been a cat genius. She taught herself, much to my chagrin, a leap and roll-over maneuver with which she snatched offending mockingbirds from the air. In spite of her apparent scrawniness, she was capable of six-foot vertical leaps. If she were sitting and staring at you, you might worry that you were being dissected. Marsha named her Hygelac in honor of a certain wise old king. We pronounced her name something like Hugh'-ghi-lack and called her Huggababy. She was affectionate but reserved. She lived twenty years.

Her sister was about as different as a sister could be. She was a gorgeous, fluffy little thing. I named her Arctiidae for a genus of moths with wooly caterpillars, although I know next to nothing about moths. The label quickly reduced to TeeDee. She had her mother's phlegmatic tendency but elevated it to an art form. If she were sitting and staring at you,

you might suspect you had wandered into her line of sight. She was affectionate and drooled profusely when petted. We took to keeping old towels about. She lived eight years.

One day, while standing in the kitchen dangling a potholder at my side, I was startled to have TeeDee jump up and take it away. This was one act she would subsequently perform on cue and it became known as TeeDee's trick. We praised her for it and she would appear to strut, seeming to really enjoy that one thing. TeeDee ate, slept, did her toilet and snatched the potholder.

A second story about TeeDee brings us back to Bubbles and her second meal in my presence. It was the day the cats became my teachers. Bubbles had gotten hungry again, so Marsha brought home another rat and put it in the terrarium. I, of course, stayed at the terrarium to see if the astonishing things I had seen last time would be repeated and confirmed. I was especially keen on the possibility of seeing the mechanism by which Bubbles generated the constricting coils around her prey.

This audience at a Bubbles feeding occurred later in the day than the previous one, so the cats were in the house for the night. I have no specific recollection of them joining me at the terrarium, but there was nothing unusual about their presence there. The terrarium sat on a large table and there was ample room, both at the ends of the table beyond the terrarium and in front of it, for the cats to sit and even

212

to sleep. At times, one or more of them slept on the glass top of the terrarium. By now, you will not be surprised to learn that, at least in my presence, the cats showed no awareness that a snake lived there.

On this occasion, I had taken up a position slightly to the left of the center of the terrarium and directly opposite the rat who had been put in at about that spot. Bubbles was to my right and already positioning herself. KihEe was at the left, sitting at an angle that put the rat on a direct line in front of him. He showed a great deal of interest in the rat, which he expressed by constant fidgeting and by touching the terrarium with his paws. TeeDee sat just to my right, also angled so that she faced the rat. Her behavior was very TeeDee-like. She was looking at (or near) the rat, but I could discern no indication that she was interested in doing anything about the rat. The rat looked towards or perhaps at Bubbles, who struck a perfect strike, pulled the rat back to her starting point and effected a couple of quick coils. From the cats' perspective, the rat may have seemed to disappear.

KihEe apparently fainted. He fell from the table and crashed to the floor. Collecting himself, he paused there momentarily, crouching like a cat with thoughts of dislodging a furball. He recovered quickly and left the scene.

Satisfied that he was all right, and turning to see what Bubbles was up to, I noticed instead that something had electrified TeeDee. Of course, little more than a foot away, Bubbles was strangling Rat, a potentially hair-raising sight. However, TeeDee was thoroughly pre-occupied with the place Rat had just been but now wasn't. TeeDee had become mesmerized by Rat's last known coordinates.

She was up from her sitting position, into an approximation of a cat stalking its prey—in spite of the fact that TeeDee had never been seen to stalk anything but the potholder—and stretched forward, long and close to the table. She peered into the rat-less void. Her muscles had even begun to quiver. At one point, her nose touched the glass front of the terrarium. She thrust her head up for an elevated view, then back down. She pulled away from the terrarium into a near-sitting position, still locked on those vexatious coordinates. TeeDee was surely looking for Rat, but never beyond the spot where she seemed to think he should be. She then turned and jumped to the floor, landed without incident and walked away. As it turned out, she was saving the best for later.

The routine of returning from work the following day was typical. I came through the side gate into the backyard and called KihEe. He came sprinting from the rear of the garden, as he almost always did, and I knelt to pet him. After a few moments of this greeting, I spotted TeeDee on the opposite side of the yard. She was occupied with a small pile of leaves under the canopy of what I recall as a Hawthorn tree. She was stretched low to the ground and quivering. Then she leapt into the air.

Thinking there must be something alive in the pile, I went to investigate, but it contained just leaves and a few twigs. I petted TeeDee, who drooled at about the expected level. I then went inside to change clothes.

A few minutes later, I returned to the backyard, ready to putter in the garden. TeeDee had crossed the yard and was under the walnut tree near the gate. She was stretched low to the ground in contemplation of a tangle of surface roots from a nearby shrub. This confrontation, too, she resolved by leaping into the air. And then it hit me. Poor little TeeDee, who was unable to see a six-foot boa in front of her eyes, was now seeing snakes everywhere she looked (or everywhere she found some surface irregularity in her environment). This behavior tailed off and was gone after a couple of days. Meanwhile, both she and KihEe continued to spend time on the table next to the terrarium where Bubbles was visibly processing Rat. One can only guess that Bubbles was a well-known irregularity and thus not visible as a leap inducer.

The trivial explanation for TeeDee's behavior is that she saw Bubbles take Rat but, being TeeDee, didn't realize what she had seen until the next day. This interpretation requires the troubling corollary that TeeDee somehow reasoned, after the fact, that there was a connection between Rat's fate and her own well-being. For example, she might have reasoned that if a snake could suddenly materialize and cause the disappearance of Rat (it was Rat's disappearance that so intrigued TeeDee), then a snake could materialize and do the same to her.

If TeeDee's reaction was the consequence of a slowly developing realization that she had seen Bubbles, KihEe's realization had to have been instantaneous. He might have reasoned something like this–"It just missed me"–before collecting himself and walking away.

There is a least one other kind of model for the cats' reactions to Bubbles. This alternative model considers two evolutionary problems simultaneously. The first problem, which we have stated before, is that the invention of the brain, and perhaps each subsequent increase in its power, had to carry with it a concomitant invention of ambiguity and hallucination. Natural Selection would have looked favorably on developments that brought these phenomena in line with the organisms' needs–i.e., the ideal brain would provide its owner with unambiguous and reality-based interpretations of data. Such a brain would recognize the truth.

The second evolutionary problem, which we apply here to non-primate mammals in particular, is the inability to see snakes. Snakes are a truth the brains of rats, cats, dogs and cows do not recognize. They can see sticks and they can see motion, but they cannot recognize a motionless snake or even one moving deliberately, positioning itself for a strike. Such mammals are so inept in this regard that one snake has found it advantageous to grow a rattle which it uses to say, "Hey, stupid, there's a snake here." It thus warns away things it does not want to eat but runs silently and invisibly in the presence of things it does want to eat. It is worth emphasizing that the mammalian blindness to snakes, while advantageous to snakes stalking dinner, can be a problem for snakes not wishing to be stepped on by something too large for dinner.

Just for fun, let us for a moment turn evolution on its head and picture Mother Nature pondering how she might provide her early mammals with a solution to their snake problem. It was too soon to consider inventing the powerful primate brain. That development, with its capability of seeing and recognizing snakes, lay millennia in the future. Her interim solution would have to be improvisation.

At the same time that she was searching for an answer to the snake problem, she was also puzzling over the tendency of her prototype mammalian brain to hallucinate. Then she remembered that this same prototype brain already had the capacity to see sudden movement—and designed an experimental solution to snakes.

Her design was to couple the deficit in the prototype—the inability to see something that's there (snakes), to the surfeit in the prototype—the ability to see something that isn't there (hallucination). The vehicle by which she would couple an invisible something to a visualized nothing was indirect and perverse. She first noted that the nervous impulse generated by detection of sudden motion had no intrinsic meaning—she could use it to trigger a sneeze or the secretion of gastric juices if she so chose. But if she were to wire it to a scary hallucination, the impulse generated by a sudden movement could be used to induce the reflex of leaping and adrenaline pumping.

Mother Nature was fully aware that this was a bizarre train of events. It made use of a lie to tell a truth. But if it helped her proto-mammal to survive, she would have time to work towards a design of a brain that could see snakes, in fact. With that satisfaction, she named the captured hallucination her Snake Picture. A hundred million years later, more or less, two cats, intent upon a rat inside a terrarium, witnessed the disappearance of that rat, in and of itself a sudden movement.

KihEe's Snake Picture went off like a strobe light. The resulting jump-adrenaline reflex was a surge off the scale and his knees buckled. "It just missed me," he reasoned, and the picture faded as he got to his feet to walk away.

TeeDee's Snake Picture warmed up like a toaster oven—hers was wired to a high impedance system. The jump-adrenaline reflex took overnight to reach threshold, and fired sporadically as the picture slowly dissipated. TeeDee reasoned, "I see a snake," because everywhere she looked, the Snake Picture was looking back at her—even when she blinked, a detail likely to have been lost on TeeDee.

If evolution really did cobble together a Snake Picture reflex as part of a system for protection against invisible predators, it would be of some interest to know its status in big-brained mammals that have since achieved the ability to see and recognize snakes. We could look for signs that a relic of the Snake Picture persists in humans and, if it does, whether there is variation in its expression.

When human meets snake, the encounter is apt to be punctuated by a relatively lively expression, such as a scream, or some other indication that the reaction is visceral in nature. Some people will follow up their initial fear and loathing by taking hold of a suitable instrument and converting the snake to mush.

I once saw a man on a golf course ruining one of his clubs in the interest of dispatching a trespassing snake. As he was bringing this heroic duty to completion, I approached the scene closely enough to see that the man was foaming about the mouth and to make out the mangled remains of a small gopher snake—one of Nature's more docile and harmless creatures (unless you're a rodent). It might help us comprehend the senseless act of lashing out at that little snake if it was reflexive–as if the man's Snake Picture had come on hot and, like KihEe's strobe light, overpowered his sensibilities. Perhaps his Snake Picture made him do it.

Putative signs of the human Snake Picture can reveal themselves in quite surprising ways. Several years ago, while standing in a supermarket check-out line, scanning the tabloids for choice revelations (the reigning champion is "The Incredible Sexual Power of Celery"), I came upon a portrait of a snake. It was accompanied by a headline story of a man who reported having been plucked from a rural road somewhere or other and taken aboard the vessel of some space aliens or other. After being variously poked and scrutinized, the story continued, he was released and was thus able to describe his ordeal. An artist, working from a description provided by the victim, sketched one of the aliens who turned out to be a snake. A spontaneous and fantastic snake sighting such as this is perhaps best understood as a manifestation of the Snake Picture. It may be that, under certain conditions, the Picture becomes too easily excitable and fires randomly. For example, in nightmares precipitated by extreme stress, the Snake Picture may revert to behaving as hallucination.

The relative excitability of the Snake Picture might even be an indicator of the stress levels in civilizations. In a truly curious development in human history, long before anyone had tumbled to the existence of fossils, and particularly dinosaur fossils, a number of different peoples (from Northern Africa to Europe and Asia) began drawing pictures of fearsome dragons—a highly stylized horse-snake hybrid with signature flame in place of tongue. We don't know the wellspring for the human invention of dragons, but the idea of a Snake Picture run amuck may deserve a look. Of course, the dragon invention might correspond to a time of intensive visitation by aliens who were dragons.

We generally ascribe the invention of ideas like dragons to imagination. Invoking imagination is arguably glib, however, because we don't really know what imagination is, with regard to either the mechanism by which it functions or the evolutionary steps by which it originated. On the other hand, we do know that imagination and hallucination bear a striking resemblance to one another. As a working hypothesis, we can propose that imagination is a controlled form of hallucination.[23] In that event, we would suppose that Natural Selection didn't deal with the problem of hallucination by eliminating it, but rather by buffering or suppressing it.

A simple way to envisage buffering or suppression of hallucination is in terms of a system that enables the brain to identify the origin of the thing it just saw. A properly functioning brain might recognize hallucinations as images arising from within and routinely quash them. A person with an active imagination might be especially adept at lowering the threshold so that hallucinations "leak" through, but in a controlled and conscious way. Coming full circle, a failure to identify an internal image as having come from within would generate an episode of hallucination. This would seem to lead to the prediction of two broad classes of hallucinogenic substances, one suppressing the identification of images, one enhancing the generation of images.

The idea that hallucination might be employed as a normal part of the functioning of mammalian brains is not especially ennobling; the Snake Picture model will be a hard sell even if true. Whatever the merits of the model, however, the modest little survey of mammalian reactions to snakes we've undertaken here points to another conclusion—one that is both compatible with the Snake Picture but also independent of it. A species like *Homo sapiens*, with a more highly evolved version of the mammalian brain, sees and recognizes things its smaller brained relatives do not. We conclude, then, that even here at the present pinnacle of mental ability, one sees another bit of evidence that the capacity to recognize- -the thing we've really been talking about all along— is a major engine of evolution.

Although grappling with the problem of hallucination has arguably advanced the cause of recognition, grappling with the companion problem of ambiguity may have played a considerably greater role. It is to ambiguity that we finally turn.

Metalog

In Which Narrator Meets Master of Ceremonies

M.C. Welcome to the big spin, David.

D. Thank you.

M.C. Uh–tell us about yourself.
You're from San Diego, correct?

D. That's correct.

M.C. And what do you do there?

D. I'm a writer.

M.C. A writer! What sorts of things do you write?

D. Oh, books. Occasional articles.

M.C. I see.
You seem to have come alone today. Do you
have a family?

D. Yes. They're at home, writing. We're all
writers.

M.C. I see. Well, perhaps they're watching?

D. I don't know.

M.C. Well, I'm sure they are, and their good
thoughts will make you a wealthy man before
you can say serendipity. So, let's,

D. Say, you wouldn't know how to spell that,
would you?

M.C. Spell? I thought you said you were a writer.

D. Well, yes, I am a writer, but I've never claimed
to be a speller.

9. The Contingency Principle

A Theory of Biological Knowledge.

There are certain properties of knowledge we can apprehend with even a lay education in the philosophical disciplines. We surely all agree, for example, that knowledge is acquired in the context of prior knowledge. Thus, even a giant like Newton must acknowledge his debt to those who came before him, and upon whose shoulders he stood. Axiom number one: knowledge builds upon knowledge.

Our second axiom will be that knowledge is contingent, subject either to verification (and re-verification) or to disproof. Even our most fervently held tenets lack immunity to attempts at disproof. The laws of Newtonian physics, for example, were abruptly called into question with the development of Einsteinian relativity. Indeed, there is a common misconception that Newtonian Law was somehow mortally wounded and then displaced by Einstein's revolution. However, even if at high velocities space is less than straight and time is less than a constant, we still know when the sun will rise and why it will do so. The Einsteinian revolution is an extension of, rather than a displacement of, the Newtonian model. Newtonian physics was incomplete but not incorrect, much as a concrete foundation can be strong when not yet a house. Einsteinian knowledge is like a nearly completed house built upon the foundation of Newtonian knowledge. Although the Newtonian world was challenged, and even rattled just a bit, it survived virtually intact.

If the foundation that was passed along to Einstein was fundamentally strong, it was because Newton and others had repaired the foundation they had inherited. They then built upon this repaired foundation. One of these repairs emerged out of the demonstration that the Ptolemaic earth-at-the-center model of the solar system made predictions that weren't borne out by observation. The Ptolemaic system—which had been embraced as canonical knowledge for fourteen centuries—was then unceremoniously discarded in favor of the Copernican (sun-at-the-center) model. The dashing of the Ptolemaic system by the likes of Copernicus, Kepler and Galileo provided a new and verified set of shoulders from which Newton looked out at the universe.

The collapse of the Ptolemaic system did not come close to a complete knowledge extinction, however. For example, orbits were a feature of that system, and these were retained in the Copernican system. The new cosmology emerged as a variation on a theme. In other words, the new knowledge still satisfied the axiomatic requirement that it be built upon prior knowledge; the knowledge continuum wasn't broken, but a branch of it was found wanting and rendered extinct. The human enterprise we call science ultimately verifies and re-verifies all of its findings and thus has the useful property of self-correction.

We should caution ourselves here that the process of verification is seldom so simple as demonstrating that something is true. It is more generally the case that an idea is elevated to the status of fact not by being proven, but by surviving disproof—it is usually difficult to prove the truth of a true idea but manageable to disprove a false idea. An idea not shown to be false may indeed be true, and if continually not shown to be false, comes to be regarded as true.

Since this could easily have the ring of sophistry, we had better consider an example; we'll use one that takes us back to biology. Early in this century there came into being the idea that genes, in those days an abstraction, were on chromosomes (the chromosome theory of heredity). Calvin Bridges, one of Morgan's students in the famous fly lab at Columbia University, showed that aberrant transmission of a particular chromosome (detected microscopically) was correlated with an aberrant inheritance pattern of a particular gene (shown genetically).

The correlated behavior of genes and chromosomes was a prediction of the chromosome theory—if a gene is on a chromosome it is constrained

226

to go where the chromosome goes. Thus, a failure to detect this correlated behavior would have doomed (negated) the theory. That the correlation was seen was consistent with the theory, which thus survived disproof. The correlation did not actually prove the theory (although Bridges claimed proof) in that both gene and chromosome could have been acting in concert with some third component which was not being monitored.

We now know, by way of abundant subsequent evidence, that the impetuous Bridges was correct. For example, it was later found that the chemical structure of genes corresponds to a part of the chemical structure of chromosomes, but not to the chemical structure of any other cellular component. Genes are made of DNA and chromosomes contain DNA. Again, if this correspondence had not been found––that is, if the chemistry of genes and chromosomes had been found to be incongruent—the chromosome theory would have been dispatched to the dustbin of unworkable ideas. Instead, by surviving another opportunity for disproof, it became even more robust. It could be called the Chromosome Law today without causing so much as a raised eyebrow.

The process we have outlined here, by which human inquiry and learning become transformed into knowledge, constitutes a modest theory of knowledge. Its three parts can be restated:

1. New knowledge builds upon prior knowledge. The nature of new knowledge is limited and influenced by the condition of the prior knowledge (Einsteinian events follow Newtonian events; the converse is disallowed).
2. Knowledge is repeatedly challenged and therefore contingent.
3. Knowledge achieves canonical or permanent status by appearing impervious to disproof; direct proof is achieved with great difficulty.

These properties of knowledge are of especial interest in the context of biology because, as we will develop below, they can also be said to be the properties of life.

We earlier portrayed the history of life as the discovery of a hierarchical series of recognitions. One step in this series is the self-recognition of informational macromolecules. Built upon that recognition is the recognition of substrates by gene products. In turn, upon that is built the recognition by single cells of the chemical features of their environments (including each other). Finally, resting on the prior levels, is the recognition by multicellular organisms of increasingly complex physical features of their environments. If we allow the premise that recognition is the biological equivalent of knowledge, then this hierarchical series of recognitions is a hierarchical system of biological knowledge. In other words, evolution consists of discovering new knowledge and integrating it with existing knowledge. Living systems consist of knowledge layered upon knowledge.

The second property of knowledge, its contingency, also has a biological cognate. New biological knowledge first appears as a proposal in the form of genetic variation. In formal terms, such variation constitutes the hypothesis that it (the variation) effects a new or improved act of recognition at one or more levels in the hierarchy of recognition. This hypothesis, upon submission to a subsequent generation, is tested by Natural Selection, which renders a judgment. Either this is a useful new function, it is an improvement upon an existing function, it makes no discernible difference or it is deleterious. The fate of the proposed new knowledge is dependent upon the direction and severity of this judgment. Moreover, the judgment can be tentative. Like the Ptolemaic solar system, some biological knowledge may persist for many generations before it is finally judged to be a poor representation of reality.

Finally, the mechanism by which genetic variation is retained is the biological cognate of validating and retaining human knowledge—it survives repudiation. Whereas human knowledge is susceptible to disproof, biological knowledge is susceptible to extinction.

If we were to adopt the point of view that evolution is a learning process—and that life is the resulting fund of knowledge—we might be led to certain reappraisals of biological phenomena. This could occur, for example, if we somehow altered the way in which we asked questions. The history of life, because it is so stubbornly resistant to experimentation, is an area in which it is particularly important to be asking the right questions.

We saw earlier that the study of evolution, a branch of historical inquiry, submits to at least indirect experimentation. One kind of experiment stems from the prediction of Neo-Darwinism that organisms which are most closely related by classical criteria, such as morphology, must also be most closely related in the sequences of subunits that occur in their informational macromolecules. This prediction has been met in a wide variety of tests. For example, human and chimpanzee DNA and proteins have been shown to be closely related to each other, as predicted, but distantly related to DNA and protein from bears and raccoons, also as predicted. Bear and raccoon DNA and protein, however, are related to each other, again, as predicted. Notice that a negative result in these experiments—if human and chimp molecules had turned out to be unrelated, for example—would have dealt Darwinism a severe blow. In other words, these kinds of experiments put Darwinian evolution to the test of invalidation. In contrast, no other model for the origin of humans and chimps makes predictions like that of molecular

230

relatedness. Such other models are, therefore, never put to the test.

When we turn our attention to extinction, which has a very complex relationship to evolution, experimental science becomes nearly impossible. One must admit that it is possible to watch the dynamics of species loss as we destroy their habitats, but this approach is evidently ill-advised. On the one hand, we have no reliable way of predicting the long-term consequences of these experiments—they have the potential to set in motion side effects which we could not see until they had already occurred, and that would be later than we might care to see them. Furthermore, if life is knowledge, and we know less than everything about the species we are destroying, their destruction is the ethical equivalent—at least—of burning books. If you are interested in an urgent and thorough treatment of the biodiversity issue, see the excellent book by Wilson (1992).

Aside from those species that are disappearing from before our eyes, the most dramatic episodes have been the so-called mass extinctions. In the Permian extinction about 250 million years ago, more than ninety percent of all marine animals perished. The timing of that event roughly corresponds to the merging of the continents to form the supercontinent Pangaea. Whether this is a cause and effect relationship we shall probably never know.

The mass extinction that really excites the imagination, however, is the one marking the end of the Cretaceous period some sixty-five million years ago. The Cretaceous extinction claimed about fifty percent of marine species and numerous terrestrial plants and animals—including the dinosaurs. It continues to amaze us that such an astonishing group of animals as the dinosaurs could completely disappear. They were not just physically incredible. Having prospered for a hundred million years, dinosaurs had also been around an incredibly long time.

The remarkable nature of dinosaurs tempts us to look for some equally remarkable explanation for their demise. But where temptation exists, experience teaches us to proceed with appropriate caution. If we are to think clearly about the end of the dinosaurs, we should consider an array of models, including an appropriately remarkable calamity model, a more benign gradualist model and an equally benign model that focuses on the adequacy of dinosaurs as biological knowledge.

The premier calamity model is well known. About sixty-five million years ago, about when the dinosaurs disappeared, a giant asteroid virtually certainly struck the earth. One scenario of possible consequences of that collision is the creation of an enormous cloud of smoke and dust, leading in turn to a sort of Cretaceous "nuclear winter" and a precipitous drop in the earth's productivity. The dinosaurs, in this scenario, are thought to have essentially starved to death.

There are at least two difficulties with this model. In the first place, lots of things, including our ancestors, survived the asteroid (i.e., it wasn't a complete anti-biological agent). It therefore seems odd that it would have killed not just some or most dinosaurs, but all of them. For comparison, try to picture an asteroid striking the earth today and killing all placental mammals but sparing various marsupials, birds, reptiles and amphibians.

The second difficulty with the calamitous asteroid model, according to some students of the subject, is the suggestion in the fossil record that dinosaurs had already been in a five- or ten-million-year decline before their total disappearance. One can imagine an asteroid contributing to dinosauran troubles, but it strains credulity to think that an asteroid was the sole cause of them.

Even if the asteroid model has weaknesses, it has one property that elevates it to the status of a scientific ideal; it makes an unambiguously clear and testable prediction. The fossil record should mark this calamity with the biggest of all bonanzas of dinosaur bones. Furthermore, the geological marker of the asteroid, the layer of iridium that represents the vaporization of the asteroid itself, should be so close to this layer of bones as to appear to cut right through it.

It is important to note here that testing this prediction will require patience. Even with millions or tens of millions of dinosaur carcasses suddenly littering the landscape—the earth, in this scenario, must have been ankle-deep in bones—only a minority of them would chance to be in fossilizing conditions. One doesn't just go into the field and dig the requisite fossils. Nonetheless, with the skill and doggedness now the norm in the field of paleontology, these fossils will one day be found (if they exist).

The classical form of gradualist model for dinosaur extinction also invokes the imposition of external causes, albeit by less dramatic avenues than a sudden drubbing from an asteroid. One variety of classical model takes note of the relationship between the timing of the dinosaurs' advances to ascendancy and the timing of the movements of continents. The beginning of the demise of dinosaurs, in the gradualist view, corresponds to the breakup of the supercontinent Pangaea by continental drift. From the end of the Jurassic, and for about eighty million years until the end of the Cretaceous, the climatic and other changes wrought by these powerful forces might have overtaken and defeated the dinosaurs. This form of gradualist model has an aesthetic appeal that's independent of its validity. If the Permian extinction marks the formation of Pangaea, and the Cretaceous extinction marks its demise, there follows a symmetrical acknowledgment of the power of geological forces.

Meanwhile, gradualist models, while seemingly reasonable, nonetheless suffer from the

234

same primary deficiency we see in calamity models. We must ask why these gradual changes killed dinosaurs and, in particular, all dinosaurs but not all amphibians, birds or mammals. It appears inescapable that if we want to understand dinosaur extinction, there is something we must first understand about dinosaurs themselves. And, of course, we have set the stage to think about dinosaurs as a system of knowledge.

By viewing dinosaurs in terms of knowledge systems, we will seek insights into their failure by changing slightly the question we ask. Instead of inquiring about what did in the dinosaurs, we will ask why it was the dinosaurs who were done in by it. The argument that will emerge is that the dinosaurs' initial success was based on a robust and dogmatic recognition of a constant set of truths about their environment. By virtue of the basis of their success, they were incapable of recognizing a contingency in their environment when they began tripping on it. It's not exactly that dinosaurs failed to adapt as their circumstances began to change. We will argue that they made the wrong adaptations and that the basis of their initial success ultimately became the basis of their undoing.

As long as we are going to talk about dinosaurs, we might as well talk about that most famous of dinosaurs, Tyrannosaurus. As one of the most—perhaps the most—fearsome of all dinosaurs, we can only picture Tyrannosaurus practicing zealous predation on other Cretaceous monsters to satisfy its healthy appetite. Who wouldn't be disappointed to learn that Tyrannosaurus was a carrion feeder?

Compare what we think about Tyrannosaurus with what we know about today's largest terrestrial predators. The grizzly bear (*Ursa horriblis* as a sign of our respect) is capable of taking large prey such as deer, but is more apt to be seen hunting berries, grubs or fish. Most human-grizzly encounters are benign— violence is most likely to result from naive campers taking snack foods into their sleeping bags at night. The bears apparently come for the snack but may, incidentally, maul the previous owner of the snack in a fit of rage that only the bears seem to understand.

Wolves, much smaller than bears but still impressive, are very fond of mice. While it is true that a pack of wolves will harry an animal as large as a moose, if the moose is healthy and strong, the wolves will go on their way—better to eat mice than go to the mat with a healthy moose. A mouse hunting wolf, like a snack chasing bear, fails to evoke the same image as Tyrannosaurus.

The least compromising of the large modern predators are the cats. As committed hunters, however, even the cats target the old, the young, the sick and the lame. To some extent, all modern predators are manicurists to the populations they prey upon. All of their feeding behaviors, from digging grubs to culling the weakest members of a herd, suggest a legacy of balance and flexibility.

236

Much as farmers put aside seed for next year's planting, modern predators leave aside the reproductives that provide continuity to their lifestyle. Indeed, it has become a staple of the conventional wisdom that modern predator-prey relationships achieve a more or less homeostatic condition, as if predator and prey were a unit of biological function.

Tyrannosaurus skeletons do not communicate to us the notion of a character who operated, with restraint, at the margins of populations of its prey—with an occasional side dish of sweet berries or succulent grubs. Instead, Tyrannosaurus had qualities that must have been predicated on the assumption of a steady supply of very large parcels of flesh. If we are not deceived by appearances, the Tyrannosaurus design did not take into account the possibility that resources might ever be limited. Tyrannosaurus was definitely not a wimp.

Tyrannosaurus Proposition Number One. On the model that life is a system of knowledge, the Tyrannosaurus book did not contain a chapter describing the consequences of contingent resources.

Beyond the virtual certainty of its ferocity, there is only one other thing we really know about Tyrannosaurus. In the long evolutionary history of the dinosaurs, Tyrannosaurus was one of the last to appear. However, it is the corollary of that timing on which we must focus. Tyrannosaurus, the most magnificent predator, was there at the end. The emergence of that incredible beast and the imminence of complete dinosauran failure may be nothing more than cosmic coincidence. But it would seem that it strains to tell us something, and we are, as always, compelled to inquire after the possibility of cause and effect.

> **Tyrannosaurus Proposition Number Two.** The selection pressures that favored the ascendancy of Tyrannosaurus, in preference to its less formidable ancestors, were a sign of trouble in dinosaur paradise.

One of the most useful things to do with any observation we would like to understand is to make a list of every conceivable hypothesis that might explain it. We can then try to think of ways to distinguish between the hypotheses—to disprove those that are inadequate. Once again, since a good deal of hypothesis testing about dinosaurs will necessarily be done with fossils as the data, we remind ourselves to proceed in a spirit of patience. It is also timely to recall that Natural Selection can only fill a need, or seize an opportunity, by acting on the genetic variation that happens to be available. In short, we need to be looking for what dinosaur bones can tell us about the nature of dinosaur variation. We will conclude that dinosaurs were unable to possess the sort of variation they ultimately needed for survival.

With these thoughts in mind, how might we explain the emergence of a predator as huge and formidable as Tyrannosaurus? There follows a sampling of hypotheses—certainly not exhaustive—that attempt to connect the arrival of Tyrannosaurus to the disappearance of dinosaurs.

<u>Hypothesis One.</u> The emergence of Tyrannosaurus led to the exploitation of a species of prey that was too large or aggressive for Tyrannosaurus' smaller ancestor. Imagine the analogy, for example, of the development over several generations of a lineage of cats able to take down elephants while the smaller ancestral form continued to focus on the likes of zebras.

Prediction one. If this expansive model were true, it would imply that things were going well for dinosaurs. It predicts that fossilized remains of Tyrannosaurus and its ancestor should be found in deposits of the same age.

Even though hypothesis one is a "good times" model, it clearly contains seeds of disaster. The new target of predation, not having had to cope with a predator until Tyrannosaurus showed up, would therefore have been confronted with a problem it did not know how to solve. The analogy of a hot knife cutting through butter would seem to apply, and extinction of the prey animal would loom as a clear and present danger. This, in turn, would call into question the long term wisdom of the Tyrannosaurus strategy of ferocity. Tyrannosaurus would more or less quickly eat itself into a pickle, and would then have to find something else to eat.

One can imagine a number of evolutionary innovations that might save Tyrannosaurus' victims from extinction. An increase in fecundity might help in the short term–although an essentially rodent strategy might be out of reach for a giant reptile.

The newly preyed upon species might also survive through break-up into subpopulations occupying only those zones of the original species range that presented some sort of physical barrier to Tyrannosaurus. Water comes to mind.

However the prey animals responded to the invention of Tyrannosaurus, it seems most likely that the response would have built upon the mechanism that kept Tyrannosaurus' ancestral population at bay in the first place. If the original animals had been too large, one would expect the initial survivors of the onslaught to be bigger; if too fast, the survivors would have to be faster; if inaccessible, the survivors would have to be more remote. These diverse strategies have a common thread––protection from Tyrannosaurus would require draconian measures and things would have become unstable in Tyrannosaurus-land.

<u>Hypothesis Two.</u> Tyrannosaurus' ancestor depleted its normal prey and vanished except that a giant variant (Tyrannosaurus) went on to exploit a new source of prey.

Prediction two. Tyrannosaurus would replace its ancestor in the fossil record. The consequences of this scenario would be much like those from hypothesis one but presumably worse. Since the initial instability would have been created by the ravages of Tyrannosaurus' ancestor, the pattern of destruction would have had an earlier beginning.

<u>Hypothesis Three.</u> Cretaceous dinosaurs were in an arms race. Cycles of increasingly formidable defenses begot more formidable weapons of attack.

Prediction three. The strata containing Tyrannosaurus fossils should also contain counterpoint fossils representing prey animals that only Tyrannosaurus could subdue. This is a prediction that virtually everyone knows has already been met. The herbivore Triceratops, one example of a Tyrannosaurus contemporary, attained a length of thirty feet, a height of eight feet and a head of seven feet, equipped with horns three or more feet in length. Triceratops is not thought to have been an easy mark, even for Tyrannosaurus.

Certain duckbilled dinosaurs, large and numerous, may have had an even better defense mechanism. Their webbed feet suggest that they could walk through, or perhaps even swim through, habitats that Tyrannosaurus could not. However, what we know about Cretaceous geology suggests that this survival technique was doomed. There was extensive mountain building during the period, with the apparent consequence of draining the previously abundant swamplands and inland seas. If duckbills had once had safe havens in these watery places, they surely lost them and, just as surely, Tyrannosaurus was presented with a picture for which it was perfectly suited—a veritable feast. We can even imagine Tyrannosaurus thriving so wildly, and gaining such an advantage in numbers, that it also began to overwhelm Triceratops. The trouble was that any such potential for feasting was necessarily temporary. We do not picture Tyrannosaurus tracking sick and lame duckbills—Tyrannosaurus would eat them all.

If Tyrannosaurus was there at the end, eating its way into oblivion, then Tyrannosaurus does more than illustrate how the dinosaur kingdom might have collapsed. That monster is also a metaphor about dinosaur evolution. The state of biological knowledge that dinosaurs had received as their legacy, and thus transmitted from generation to generation in their attempt at continuity of that legacy, was apparently monolithic. The genetic variation that the dinosaur line submitted to Natural Selection always seems to have solved survival quandaries in the same way; they typically enhanced or even exaggerated whatever had worked for them in the past. One of the

242

ways this repeatedly manifested itself was through what now strikes us as astonishing size.

Virtually everything one might think about Tyrannosaurus contains an element of instability. This commonality leads us to a succinct model for dinosaur extinction, outlined here in three parts:

1. Life is a system of knowledge and dinosaurs represented a particular branch of this knowledge. They were what their lineage had learned about life.
2. Tyrannosaurus was the most magnificent predator ever to walk the earth but was the response of its lineage to resources that were actually dwindling—even if there appeared to be a bounty.
3. Dinosaurs committed suicide by making exactly the wrong responses to the stresses confronting them.

The fundamental flaw in the dinosaur system of biological knowledge was a blindness to the contingent nature of their resources. As an analogy, imagine humans building a machine to, say, harvest old growth forest because it had become increasingly more difficult to get to what little was left. The machine would create the initial impression that supplies were plentiful but would soon be out of work.

The contingency model for dinosaur extinction has a corollary. Organisms that managed to survive, while dinosaurs were becoming extinct, must have had a form of biological knowledge that was either immune to or else accounted for the same set of contingencies that was killing the dinosaurs. We can assume that most bacteria, for example, were immune. There is one group of organisms, though, that has attributes which seem to account for contingency. That group, of course, is the mammals.

There is a peculiar folly that creeps into our thoughts about mammals *vis-à-vis* dinosaurs. It is a commonplace, during bouts of amazement over dinosaurs, for a statement of the following sort to emerge: dinosaurs were the dominant form of life for a hundred million years, whereas humans have been the dominant form for much less than a million years. Such statements are often preceded or followed by an admonition to the effect that we human upstarts should be circumspect about our prospects. If organisms as successful as dinosaurs can perish, presumably anything can perish and arrogance is contraindicated.

While it is surely fine advice to guard against arrogance, it is nonetheless invalid to compare all dinosaurs to just one mammal. If we instead consider all of mammalian history, the record stretches back some one hundred and ninety million years. The last sixty-five million of those years have witnessed a mammalian success on a par with that of dinosaurs.

244

Ironically, mammalian success probably owes its origins as much to the dinosaurs as to any other factor.

Before the Cretaceous extinction, mammals tended to be small, nocturnal and underground. Their fund of knowledge represented the outcome of their experiments with survival in environments out of the dinosaurs' way. In other words, the central theme in the early evolution of mammalian biological knowledge was not concerned with surging ahead like the dinosaurs, but with making do with resources around the edges of the vertebrate theater. Mammals arose as students of the contingent margins, which may help to explain how mammals came to be the masters of contingency that they are today. Mastery of contingency is a form of knowledge that necessarily built first upon the recognition of contingency itself, and then upon the discovery of survival techniques that employ the accommodation of contingency. A likely environment in which such recognition and discovery would have enormous selective value is one that puts a premium on flexibility and compromise, as in being underfoot when the likes of Tyrannosaurus is towering overhead.

The primary manifestation of these contrasting interpretations of the environment—the robust (non-contingent) interpretation by dinosaurs and the more tentative (contingent) interpretation by mammals—should be found within the mechanism used to generate the interpretations. A given dinosaur apparently had a single model of its world. Under duress, Natural Selection could tweak this model, but fundamental change was not possible. The innovation Mother Nature seems to have discovered in her mammalian experiments was a method to allow multiple models of the environment to co-exist. Since biological problem solving is essentially the process of finding a model of the environment that fits the existing circumstances, an organism that survives changeable and oscillating environments will be one that has multiple models of the environment and can switch between and among them. Thus, we might picture the confrontation between a pack of wolves and a moose to employ model switching something like this.

1. Wolves see moose; moose-meat model lights up. In human language, the message is, "Let's eat that moose."
2. In the present case, the moose is strong and healthy and offers to break wolf bones with his mighty antlers. The wolves can feel the wind. The moose-meat model shuts off as the broken wolf bone model lights up.
3. The alpha wolf makes a command decision and departs in the direction of a nearby meadow where mouse hunting has traditionally been good. The rest of the pack follows eagerly.

246

This scenario is derived from the observation that when wolves encounter a moose, they clearly take its measure. But if they approach a moose as if they would eat it, and then depart from the moose as if they prefer mice anyway, have they, as we are inclined to say, changed their minds? One view of mind changing was expressed by the fictional character Spock––when asked, with regard to a particular decision, if he wouldn't change his mind, he inquired if there were something wrong with the one he had. Although we realize that the author of that exchange was having fun with literal interpretation of figurative speech, we are also reminded that the notion that minds change is, itself, figurative. Perhaps we can muster a more operational description of what occurs during a mind change. As a corollary, we would like to know what is in place when a mind has finished changing—when it is made up. What is the state of a made up mind, and what change of state characterizes the process of becoming made up?

It helps to go back to the origin of mind. The single cell master chemists began laying the foundation of mind half a billion years ago. After tumbling to the invention of multicellular existence, they began to re-invent themselves as physicists. The mind is the modern derivative of organisms learning the physics of life, first by learning to detect physical signals from the surroundings and then by learning advantageous responses to those signals. In modern organisms like mammals, this process has become extraordinarily elaborate.

As an example, when a wolf hears, sees and smells a moose, the wolf has received signals in the form of sound waves generated by the moose, light waves that bounced off the moose and olfactibles released by the moose (the latter is actually a chemical signal). These signals are transformed into a representation of the moose. That is, signals emanating from the moose are transformed into a mental representation or image of the moose. We know this transformation occurs, even if we are years and perhaps decades from an understanding of the mechanism by which it is accomplished. Moreover, if the wolf is hungry, the transformed representation makes intimate contact with the wolf's salivary glands, among other things. The moose is recognized as edible. In contrast, if the moose is aggressive, it is transformed into a different representation that tends to make less intimate contact with the salivaries and more intimate contact with the adrenal cortex. The moose is recognized as dangerous and the taste in one's mouth is fear, not moose.

We propose, then, that a wolf harbors at least two representations of moose. Upon encountering a moose, the wolf scans this small bank of possible models of moose to determine which model this particular moose matches. Rather than a change of mind, the decision reflects the selection of the best available model to fit current circumstances. Whether

248

wolves are capable of other representations of moose we do not know. Humans, however, surely have additional models of moose, from barometer of an ecosystem to a poet's inspiration.

The observation that mammalian minds contain multiple representations of unitary objects may seem of no great moment when viewed in isolation. However, when we view this property of mind in the full context of life's history, we sense that we've seen this before. Indeed we have. The trick of multiple representations of a unitary object was first discovered by single cells. At the pinnacle of their sophistication, single cells had learned how to represent themselves in many different ways, depending upon the circumstances in which they find themselves. Recall, for example, that in the course of human embryological development, the same cell ultimately represents itself as more than two hundred cell types. In this developmental manifestation, we referred to multiple representations as the product of contingency chemistry.[24] By analogy, the mental capacity for multiple representations of unitary objects is the product of contingency physics.

The finding that evolution has discovered contingency in both the chemical and physical manifestations of biological systems, and that these discoveries occupy crossroads in evolutionary history, suggests a principle is at work here. Such a principle may be at the heart of what we yearn to understand about life.

10. A Role for Life in the Universe

The known universe is described in terms of just two classes of properties—the chemical and the physical—and its entire history is chronicled with respect to these properties alone. The history of life, at least on this planet, is the saga of mastering these properties. The earliest part of life's history unfolds as a series of discoveries of increasingly complex chemical recognitions or truths. These truths reached their zenith in contingency, which manifests itself as the ability of single cells to recognize the multifaceted nature of their immediate environments, and to interact with those environments by being multifaceted in turn. The chemical behavior of a particular cell is contingent upon the chemistry of the place in which it finds itself. It is precisely the discovery of chemical contingency that bridges the transition from single-celled to multicelled life forms. Mother Nature occupied herself as chemist for some three billion years.

The more recent history of life, a period covering the last 500 million years, more or less, chronicles discoveries of increasingly complex physical truths. These truths, too, reached their zenith in contingency—the ability to take the measure of the same distant object in different ways. Wolves take the measure of a moose—whether it's dinner or it's dangerous. Their capacity to do this is a fine-

250

tuned derivative of the senses that recognize physical information in the environment.

The litany of recognitions, from the origin of life to the present, is simple even if the mechanisms of these recognitions are not:

Mastery of chemistry-based recognition .
Discovery of contingency chemistry.
Discovery of physics-based recognition .
Discovery of cntingency physics.

This litany constitutes a hierarchy of recognitions and simultaneously describes the continuum of life from its inception. Moreover, the inception itself is based upon the recognition of atoms and molecules that are by-products of the life and death cycles of stars, thus putting the continuum of life squarely into the continuum of the universe.[24]

Once a lineage reaches the level of contingency physics and starts down the road of multiple modeling, there follows enormous selective advantage in an increased capacity for the storage and manipulation of those models—in other words, advantage in a larger brain. This stands in dramatic contrast to the *T. rex* strategy which was predicated on a larger lizard. Whereas selection pressure for larger lizards has one form of severe constraint—an infinitely large lizard is out of the question—selection pressure for a larger brain has a different constraint—

one presumes that pressure can occur only to the point of selecting a brain capable of generating all possible models of all possible universes. The capacity to generate an infinite number of models, and thus to recognize all possible universes, may already be within human grasp. An easily overlooked consequence of possessing infinite models is that one of them must be the model of oneself, a rough description of consciousness.

A lineage on the path of multiple modeling would find companion advantage associated with improvements in the actual assembly of models. Some models, like the Snake Picture proposed earlier, can be thought of as congenital, thus requiring little or no assembly. As a model of the environment, the Snake Picture would consist of some variation of the hypothesis that the environment has the capacity to produce materializations, coupled to the interpretation that materializations are dangerous. An accidental expression of the model would create a materialization where there was none, pointing up the importance of fidelity in the mechanism that controls expression. Hallucinations can be just as hazardous as unannounced appearances.

Most models are not employed to precipitate simple reflex reactions, however, and, indeed, most models are not congenital. Although we do not understand the neurobiology of model building or model switching, we know a good deal about some of the behaviors associated with these activities. We will

252

trouble ourselves here with a single facet of that behavior, the well-known phenomenon that mammals nurture their young in proportion to the extent of their modeling capacity (this relationship is expressed classically in terms of time of nurturing versus size of brain).

Animals like wolves, with a moderate number of models to show their young spend a moderate amount of time schooling their young. Animals like humans, with bigger brains and more models, devote a much longer time to teaching and learning. One of the key steps in the acquisition of model generating capacity, in the human lineage in particular, was the discovery that derivative models can be created by using combinations of existing models—a rough description of thought and imagination. Learning this art of derivation is probably what takes us humans so long to grow up.

It cannot hurt to remind ourselves that modern model building, including consciousness and rational thought, springs from the 500 million-year-old experiment in the recognition and rationalization of physical signals from the environment. This places the constructs we call consciousness and thought squarely within the long continuum of biological experimentation.

But what might it all mean? If chemical contingency constitutes the shoulders upon which life stood to begin its exploration of physics, does contingency in physics, in turn, offer its broad shoulders as a place for life to stand, and thereby see further still? Perhaps our best clue comes from returning for a moment to the measures of a gene in these levels of organization. In chemical contingency, the measure is direct, in physical contingency, it is indirect. Beyond that point, the measure is abstract and only discernible in the context of the prior measures. This would have profound implications, especially for the way we educate our children. That will be the topic for another time and place.

Epilog

In the beginning there was Truth,
seamless but for the Question,
a Ripple on the Universe of Truth,
and the seam was essence and particle of Truth.

Thus came Recognitions and the Ones that are Life
looked to the future that they might inform the past.
For the Origin held Truth but no Knowledge,
while Life acquires Knowledge and becomes Truth.

So Life is not mystery after all but Answer,
marking endless Time and
reveling in the Infinity of
Contingent Universes.

1. Most of the dating of fossils like the stromatolites exploits the slow decay of uranium (through some fourteen steps) to yield a rare isotope of lead. In a sample, the ratio of uranium to the rare isotope of lead provides an extremely accurate measure of the sample's age.

2. Eukaryotic cells, like ours, have a true nucleus; a membrane separates the genetic material (chromosomes) from the rest of the cell. Prokaryotic cells, such as bacteria, lack this compartment. The evolutionary divergence between eukaryotic and prokaryotic cells occurred more than a billion years ago.

3. Schrödinger's description of an "aperiodic crystal" was written about proteins as the likely genetic material, a common theme in his day. However, his description of the properties of this crystal is a nearly perfect description of the salient properties of DNA. His use of a Morse code analogy is an uncanny anticipation of the triplet code, discovered some 30 years later.

4. Genes, although not necessarily of DNA, are actually a prediction of Darwinian evolution in that it requires information that is variable and transmitted

from generation to generation. Transmitted, variable information is a decent description of what genes are.

5. Not all genes are named after the phenotype associated with mutant alleles. The genes that encode the hemoglobins, for example, are called the hemoglobin genes. If they had been named after mutant alleles they would have names reflecting the anemia that would be associated with the mutant forms. This represents a type of special case in which an easily obtainable cell type (red blood cells) is also chock-full of one type of protein (hemoglobins). The ability to recover large amounts of the protein in pure form allowed extensive biochemical analysis of the protein without regard to the gene that encodes the protein.

Biochemists were also able to characterize many enzymes without recourse to genetic analysis. They devised elaborate purification schemes to isolate this class of molecules for study. Consequently, when genes encoding these enzymes were found, they could be named after the normal enzyme rather than after the phenotypic effects the mutant forms had on the organism.

6. It takes two in sexually outcrossing species. Bacteria, for example, can tango solo.

7. In some instances, a pair is not enough of a group. One of the problems encountered in efforts to save

endangered species is that of effective gene pool size. If a population has been decimated too severely, it may continue to decline simply because there are too few individuals to maintain a requisite level of outcrossing.

8. In the first part of this paragraph, we ignore systems that repair damage to DNA, but this does not affect the argument. Also, cell division by fission in prokaryotes and by mitosis/meiosis in eukaryotes are quite different in details. However, each contains the essential elements of semi-conservative replication of DNA followed by partition of the daughter DNA molecules into daughter cells. In this respect, the two systems are identical.

9. As an alternative, it is possible that fecundity equals transmissibility and longevity equals mutability. The third comparison would then have to be the incongruous one that information equals fidelity. The form of the argument that would follow from this alignment would still be that *The Selfish Gene* muddies the waters by ignoring the fundamental property that genes are information.

10. There are circumstances that seem not to conform to the behavior outlined here with arcane names like heterosis and balanced lethal systems. They do not, however, contravene the principle that Natural

Selection patiently monitors variation, one functional gene at a time.

11. There are small peptides that are synthesized enzymatically–i.e., without an RNA message. Most of these are antibiotics produced by various bacterial species and are no more than ten amino acids in length. Actinomycin D is an example.

12. In keeping with the richness of life, there are exceptions to this rule. Cells of the immune system, for example, are terminally differentiated but retain their capacity to divide if given the proper stimulation. Indeed, this property is fundamental to the immune response.

13. The scheme in Appendix 6 also shows a transmembrane protein. A large variety of such proteins engage in functions ranging from the transport of metabolites like sugars across membranes to receiving and transmitting signals, such as those carried by hormone molecules synthesized in other cells.

14. It is precisely in this activity that plants and algae also capture molecules of carbon dioxide from the atmosphere. Thus, sugar production by plants reduces the concentration of CO_2. Sugar combustion, which is what occurs when we breathe or operate

internal combustion engines, releases this greenhouse gas.

15. ATP is utilized to attach the amino acids to their respective amino-acyl-tRNA-synthetases (i.e., to charge the tRNAs), and its close relative GTP (guanosine triphosphate) is used to bring the charged tRNAs into the A-site on the ribosomes.

16. The phenomenon of simultaneous enablement and constraint appears elsewhere in Darwinian thought. You may recall its use in the discussion of group selection. In that context, the necessity for a group is seen as enabling and constraining Natural Selection.

17. The original condition, a single attachment site in a haploid nucleus, would require that the attachment site be related to the division axis of the cell. The creation of a diploid cell would generate a nucleus with two attachment sites. If there remains a single axis of division (which is necessary in order that these ancient experiments yielded today's diploid descendants), then we picture the two attachment sites as being adjacent and in tandem on the midpoint of this axis.

18. We can picture the attachment of the chromosome of modern bacteria to their plasma membrane as analogous to the idea of a single place at

the midpoint of the axis of division. If the attachment site were detached from the membrane and became an appurtenant structure of the chromosome, followed by association with independent fibers of the spindle instead of the membrane, room is created for an additional chromosome in the division apparatus. Reversion to unstable diploid mitosis–i.e., to meiosis–could then be achieved via a controlled mechanism that causes the division to initiate under the primitive condition of attachment to the membrane. Given a mechanism to switch between the two types of chromosome behavior, the stage is set for the evolution of modern meiosis.

19. One could construct a similar model in which the first diploids divided *via* normal mitosis from the beginning and evolved a system of attachment site rotation running counter to the one proposed here. The model that diploid mitosis represents the suppression of meiosis is preferred for reasons alluded to in the text.

20. Some single-celled organisms produce spores which, by way of dormancy, give a sense of discontinuity across time.

21. The developmental segmentation seen in an organism like Drosophila is initiated in the egg but depends also upon the zygotic expression of other genes in the developmental cascade. This may

provide an important clue to the origin of the Cambrian explosion. As Gould has pointed out, the organisms of the explosion have the appearance of being closely related, as if they originated from a single type not long before the known specimens became entrapped and fossilized. As a working hypothesis, imagine that the Ediacaron or similar fauna represents the invention of the egg, and that this fauna contains variable individuals.

Given the existence of the egg, the invention or introduction of zygotically expressed segmentation functions would create a two-stage system.. Since the egg-borne morphogens and the zygote-borne segmentation products are both DNA binding proteins, we can imagine them to be related by the well-known phenomenon of gene duplication and divergence. If the segmentation functions are also diverse and begin to spread through the diverse population of egg producers, the derived diversity would appear combinatorial and explosive.

22. An alternative possibility is raised by evidence that the zygotic centrosome is donated by the male gamete (Simerly *et al*, 1995). The egg, in this scenario, donates everything but the centrosome and the sperm sheds everything but the centrosome, perhaps providing a vehicle by which the sperm nucleus finds its way to the egg nucleus.

262

23. There is an analogy of sorts, from the world of industry, to the model of imagination as a controlled form of hallucination. Arc welding (which, like imagination, can be productive) is a controlled form of short-circuiting (which, like hallucination, creates problems).

24. The diploid exploratory phase of multicellular organisms is also contingent, escaping to the form of its haploid progenitor via meiosis.

25. The litany of recognitions that describe biology also extend to the matter of the universe: molecules are combinations of the inter-recognitions of atoms which are combinations of inter-recognitions of sub-atomic particles. The production, by exploding stars or supernovae, of increasingly complex atoms essential for life, has led Carl Sagan and others to describe us chemically as star-stuff.

BIBLIOGRAPHY

Alexander, R. and P. Sherman. 1977. Science 96: 494-500.

Campbell, N. 1993. *Biology*, Third Edition. Redwood City: Benjamin/Cummings.

Cech, T. 1986. Scientific American 255(5): 264-275.

Dawkins, R. 1976. *The selfish gene* (New Edition, 1989). Oxford: Oxford University Press.

Fulton, C. 1977. Annual Review of Microbiology 31: 597-629.

Gould, S. 1989. *Wonderful life.* New York: W. W. Norton.

Houghton, R. 1993. Trends in Genetics 9: 235-239.

Horowitz, N. 1961. In Bryson, V. and H. Vogel (eds.), *Evolving genes and proteins.* New York: Academic Press.

Leaky, R. and R Lewin. 1992. *Origins reconsidered.* New York: Doubleday.

Margulis, L. 1981. *Symbiosis in cell evolution.* San Francisco: W. H. Freeman.

Miller, S. and L. Orgel. 1974. *The origins of life on earth.* Englewood Cliffs: Prentice-Hall.

Muller, H. 1922. American Naturalist 56: 32-50.

Ohno, S. 1971. *Evolution by gene duplication.* New York: Springer-Verlag.

Platt, J. 1964. Science 146: 347-353.

Rebek. J. 1994. Scientific American 271(1): 48-55.

Schrödinger, E. 1944. *What is Life?* Cambridge: Cambridge University Press.

Simerly, C. and others. 1995 Nature Medicine 1(1):47-
    52.
Stent, G. 1966. In Cairns, J., G. Stent and J. Watson
    (eds.), *Phage and the origins of molecular biology.*
    Cold Spring Harbor: Cold Spring Harbor Press.
Trivers, R. and H. Hare. 1976. Science 191: 249-263.
Wilson, E. 1992. *The diversity of life.* Cambridge:
    Belnap Press.

APPENDIXES

Appendix 1. <u>Chemical subunits of DNA and the Nature of Base Pairing</u>. Nucleic acids are polymers containing carbon-nitrogen ring compounds known as bases, Thymine, Cytosine, Adenine and Guanine. These are attached to sugars—ribose in RNA and deoxyribose in DNA. A short stretch of DNA is shown in (a). The diagram here is in an artificial, non-helical configuration to show clearly the hydrogen bonds (wavy lines), a primary means by which the halves of the double helix are held together. From top to bottom, left to right this example shows base pairs TA-GC-AT-CG.

(a)

   The relationship of the two strands of the helix is shown in (b). The rings of the purine and pyrimidine bases are shown as lines since they would be seen edge-on from this angle. A nanometer (nm) is one billionth of a meter.

   In RNA, uracil is used in place of thymine and ribose in place of deoxyribose (c). The hydroxyl group (-OH) at the position labeled "2" is replaced by a hydrogen (-H). RNA molecules are generally single stranded but certain types, such as transfer RNAs (tRNAs), contain fold-backs or hairpins, stabilized by paired, hydrogen bonded regions similar to DNA. An illustration of this is shown in Appendix 3.

A1

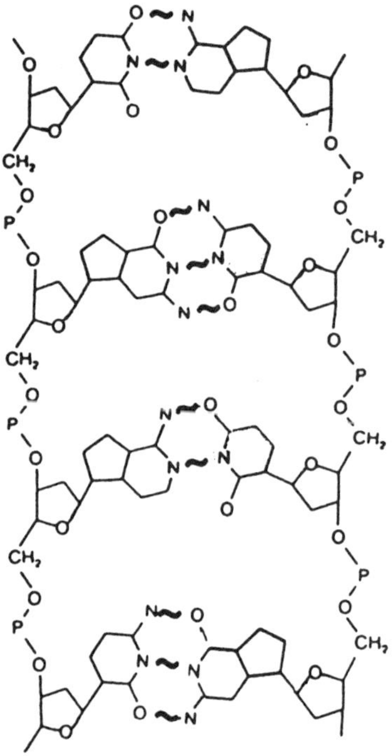

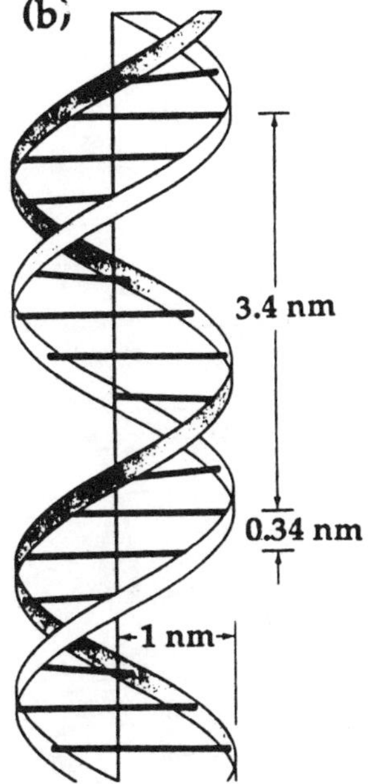

(c)

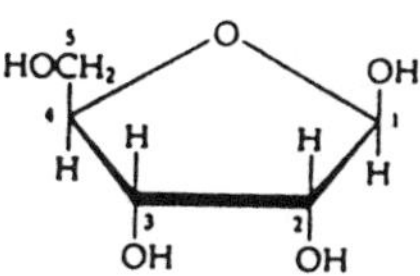

Ribose in RNA
(replaces deoxyribose)

Uracil in RNA
(replaces Thymine)

Appendix 2 Legend. <u>Overview of Mitosis and Meiosis</u>. Mitotic division can occur in either haploid or diploid cells—notice that the two chromosomes illustrated do not interact. In contrast, miosis requires diploidy—each chromosome must be paired with a homolog.

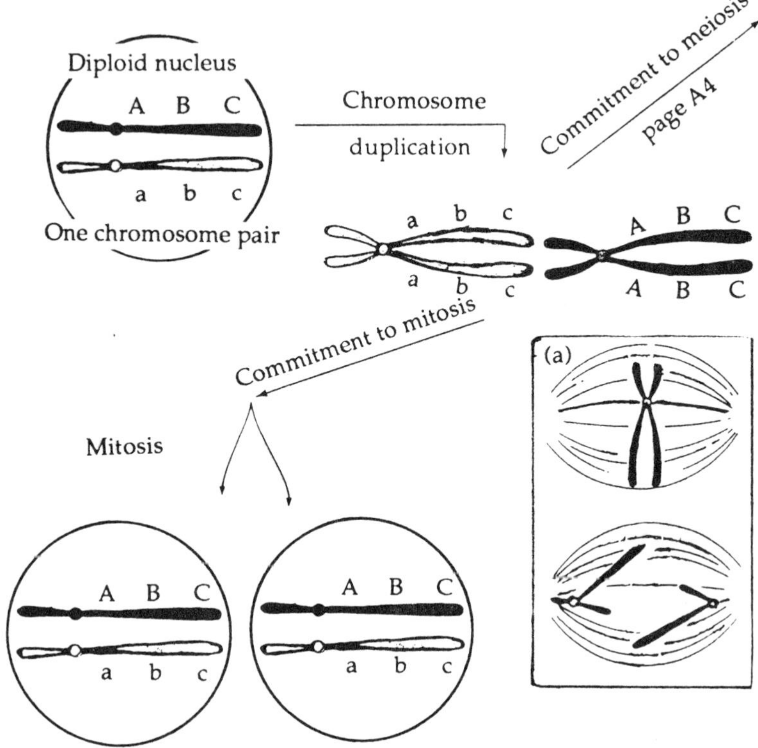

Two identical diploid nuclei

The inset at (a) illustrates the relationship of a chromosome to the spindle apparatus of a dividing cell. The inset at (b) illustrates the consequences of chiasma formation which may occur at any one of many point along the length of the chromosome. In a given cell, the position of the resulting exchange of chromosome parts is identical in each homolog and neither is augmented nor diminished in the process

A3

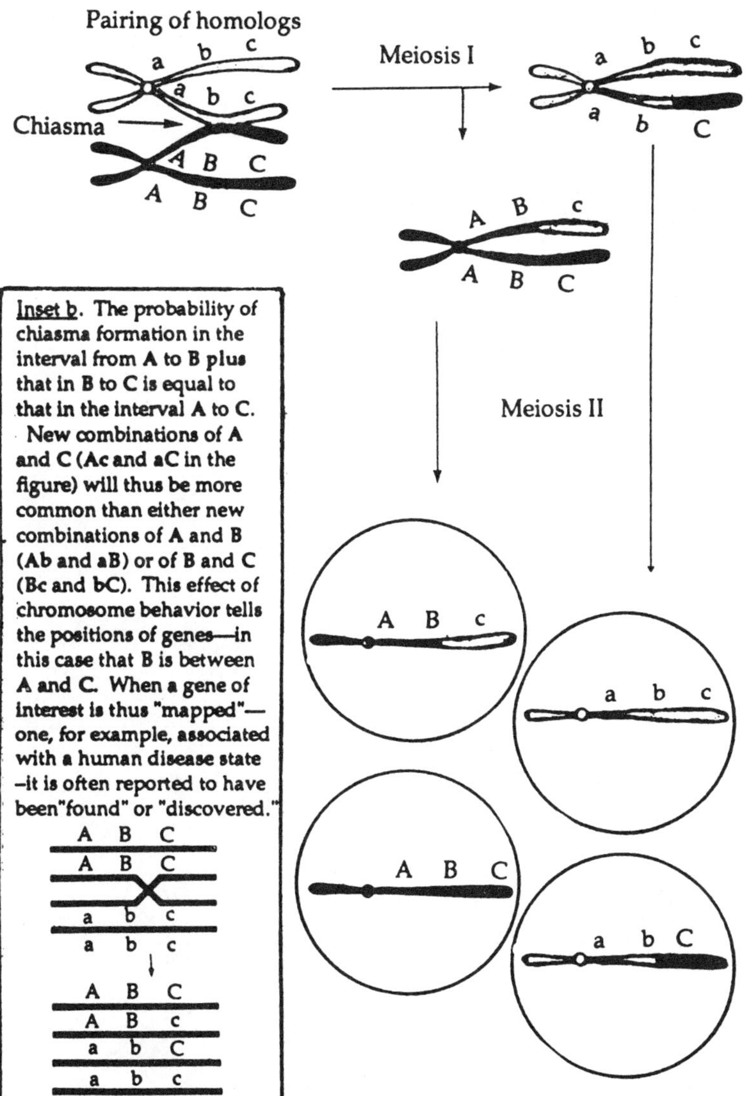

<u>Inset b</u>. The probability of chiasma formation in the interval from **A** to **B** plus that in **B** to **C** is equal to that in the interval **A** to **C**. New combinations of **A** and **C** (**Ac** and **aC** in the figure) will thus be more common than either new combinations of **A** and **B** (**Ab** and **aB**) or of **B** and **C** (**Bc** and **bC**). This effect of chromosome behavior tells the positions of genes—in this case that **B** is between **A** and **C**. When a gene of interest is thus "mapped"— one, for example, associated with a human disease state —it is often reported to have been "found" or "discovered."

Four non-identical haploid nuclei.

A4

Appendix 3. <u>Amino acids and transfer RNAs</u> Panel **(a)** shows the twenty amino acids from which proteins are constructed, arranged approximately by length of side chain or "R" group. The R groups of Glycine (H) and Alanine (CH_3) are indicated by arrows. The biological activity of a protein depends upon its amino acid content. For example, Lysine occurs frequently in proteins that bind DNA (the positively charged R group is electrostatically compatible with negatively charged DNA molecules).

(a)

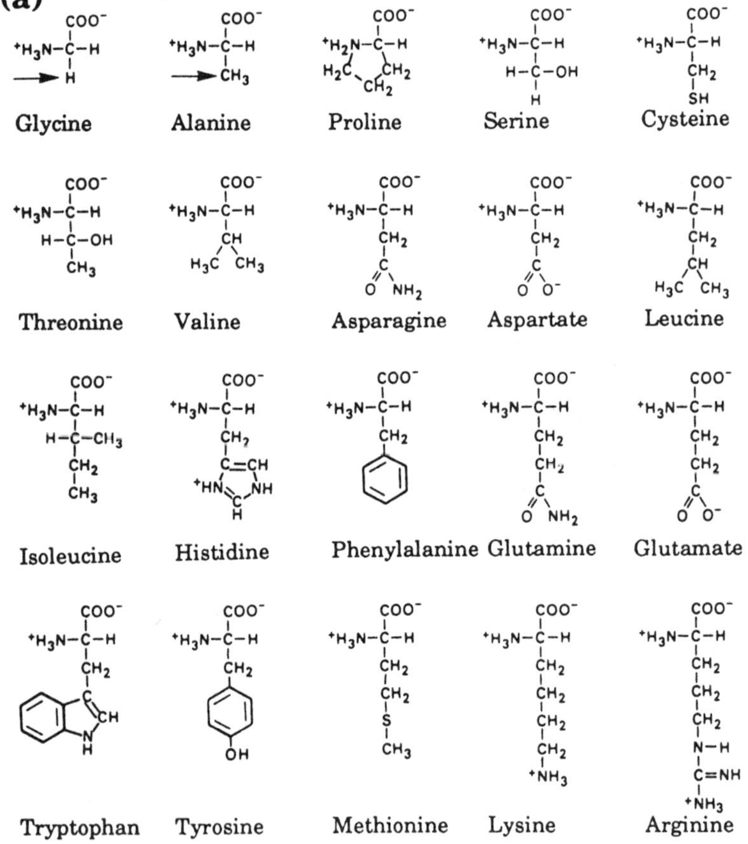

Glycine	Alanine	Proline	Serine	Cysteine
Threonine	Valine	Asparagine	Aspartate	Leucine
Isoleucine	Histidine	Phenylalanine	Glutamine	Glutamate
Tryptophan	Tyrosine	Methionine	Lysine	Arginine

A5

Panel **(b)**. All proteins are linear polymers of amino acids.
The first step in synthesis is the joining of two amino acids to create
a <u>dipeptide</u>. Additions to the peptide occur by joining the amino
(NH_3) terminus of each successive amino acid to the carboxy (COO^-)
terminus of the growing chain. The mechanism of synthesis is
shown in more detail in Appendix 4.

Dipeptide formation

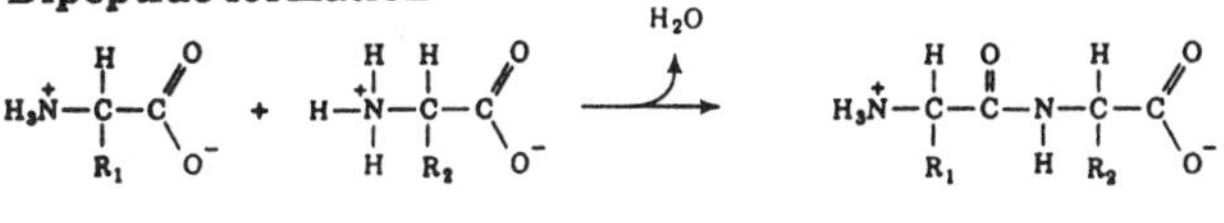

Tripeptide formation

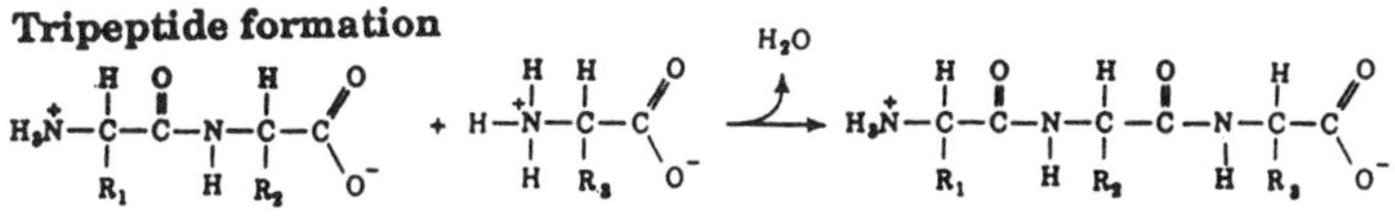

Panel **(c)**. Transfer RNA (tRNA) molecules play a central role
in the translation of information from nucleic acids to protein
(Appendix 4). A typical tRNA is a single strand of RNA (see
Appendix 1) about 75 nucleotides in length , compactly folded and
stabilized by internal hydrogen bonding (dashes in the figure at the
left, below). Each tRNA has an anticodon loop with a specific triplet
of nucleotides and a specific amino acid attached at * (below, right).

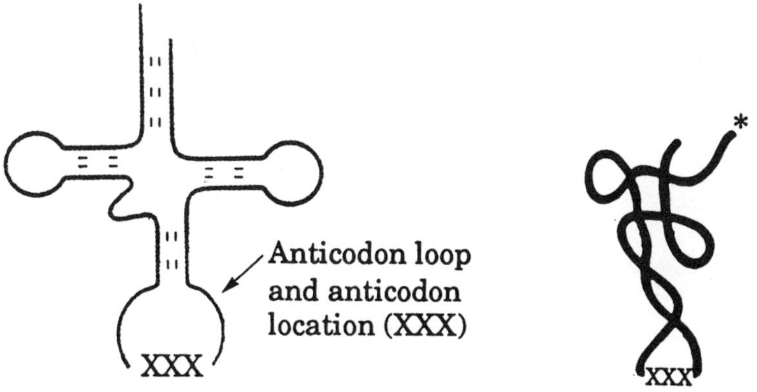

Anticodon loop
and anticodon
location (XXX)

A6

Appendix 4. <u>An Outline of Protein Synthesis</u>. Messenger RNA (mRNA) is transcribed from one strand of a DNA double helix, beginning at a promoter and ending at a specific site as described in the text. In eukaryotes, the RNA transcript is modified (not shown) and transported (2) to the cytoplasm where it is joined by a ribosome and a tRNA charged with the amino acid methionine (3, 4). The tRNA occupies a specific location on the ribosome called the P-site. A second charged tRNA joins this initiation complex in the A-site of the ribosome (5). In this example, the A-site is occupied by the triplet codon UUU. The tRNA must have the complementary anticodon AAA; this tRNA is always charged with phenylalanine by the corresponding amino-acyl-tRNA-synthetase (6).

Once the second tRNA is in the A-site, an enzymatic activity (peptidyl transferase) on the ribosome (symbolized by †) catalyzes the formation of a peptide bond between the two amino acids (7), causing the release (8) of the tRNA from the P-site. The tRNA in the A-site, still hydrogen-bonded to the mRNA, then ratchets into the P-site (9). The new triplet simultaneously ratcheted into the A-site now serves to guide the appropriate tRNA and its attached amino acid into place by the mechanism in (5). The process continues until a termination codon (UAA, UAG OR UGA) enters the A-site, synthesis terminates, the protein chain is released and the ribosome-mRNA complex disassembles. The process can restart at (3).

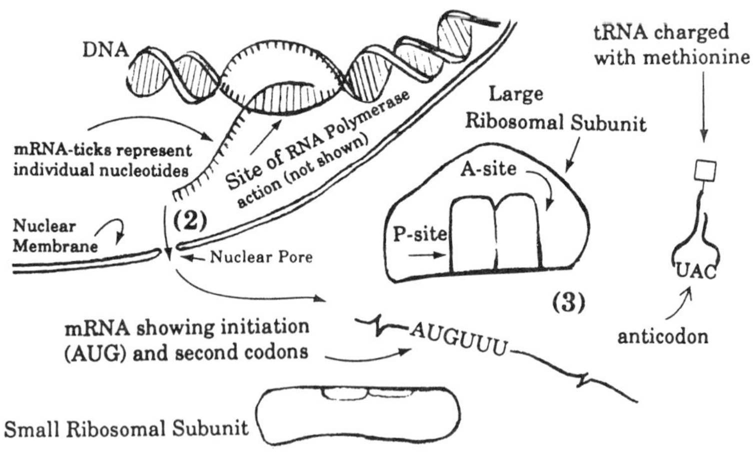

A7

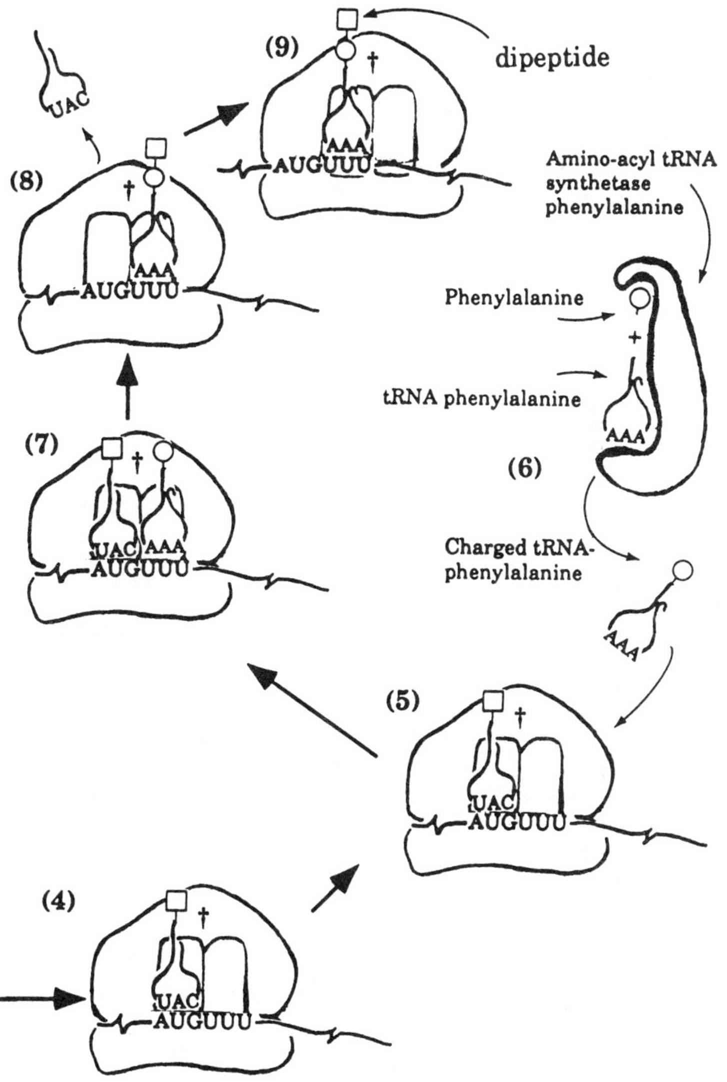

(9)
dipeptide
UAC
(8)
AUGUUU
AAA
Amino-acyl tRNA
synthetase
phenylalanine
Phenylalanine
tRNA phenylalanine
AAA
(6)
(7)
UAC AAA
AUGUUU
Charged tRNA-
phenylalanine
AAA
(5)
UAC
AUGUUU
(4)
UAC
AUGUUU
A8

Appendix 5. <u>Pyrimidine Biosynthesis</u>. Pyrimidine ring manufacture is typical of biological syntheses—the individual steps do not occur spontaneously but require the action of biological catalysts, enzymes encoded in genes, which are indicated in bold type on bold arrows in the figure. The addition of the sugar ribose (see Appendix 1) to the pyrimidine ring, which occurs between the conversion of orotate to uracil, has been omitted to focus attention on the relative simplicity of pyrimidine ring manufacture.

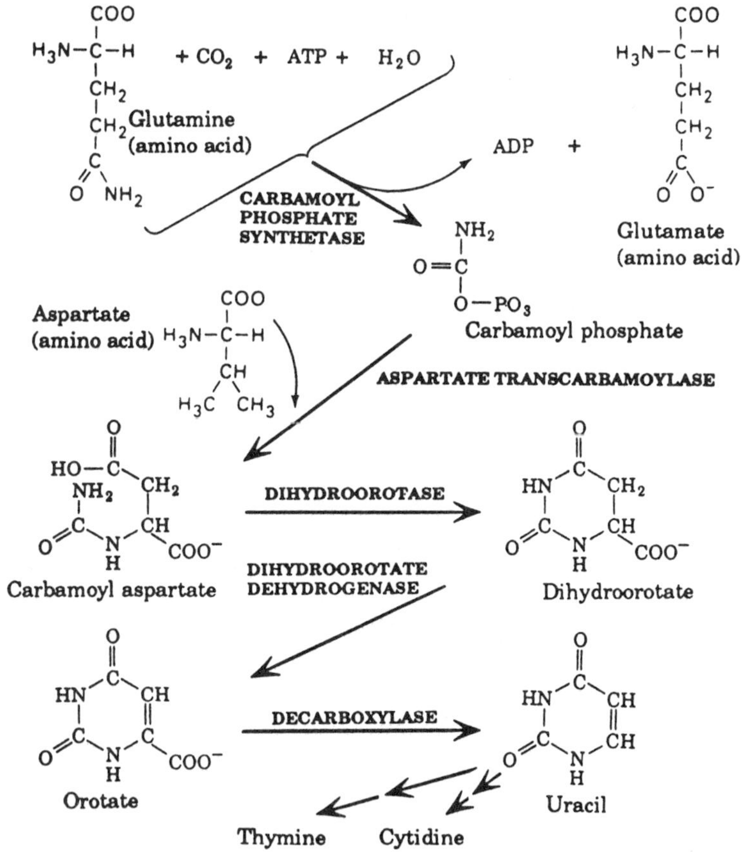

Appendix 6. <u>Cell membranes</u>. The structural formula of phosphatidyl choline, one of the common phospholipids in cell membranes, is shown in (a). Notice the carbon-carbon double bond in one of the long fatty acid chains; such <u>unsaturated</u> chains have a kink at the site of the double bond, shown diagrammatically in (b). The resulting configuration prevents neighboring molecules from packing tightly, as shown in (c), rendering the membrane fluid and flexible. A cell has a complete "skin" of lipid bilayer analogous to the skin of a basketball. However, through use of internal supports and connections, cells assume myriad shapes and are rarely spherical. Cells also have many inclusions in their membranes, especially proteins of a variety of shapes and functions (d).

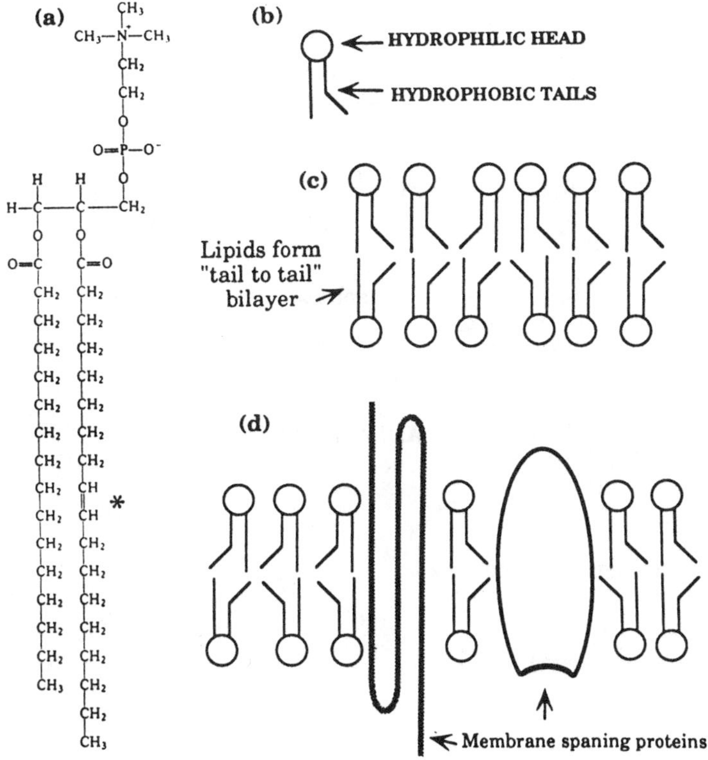

Appendix 7. **Biological energy.** Cellular work is powered by the energy cyclically stored in and retrieved from chemical bonds such as the "high energy bonds" (*) of ATP—adenosine triphosphate. The energy is tapped for some purposes by hydrolyzing the terminal bond; for other reactions, the sub-terminal bond is hydrolyzed. The relationship of this energy currency to sugar metabolism is shown, highly simplified.

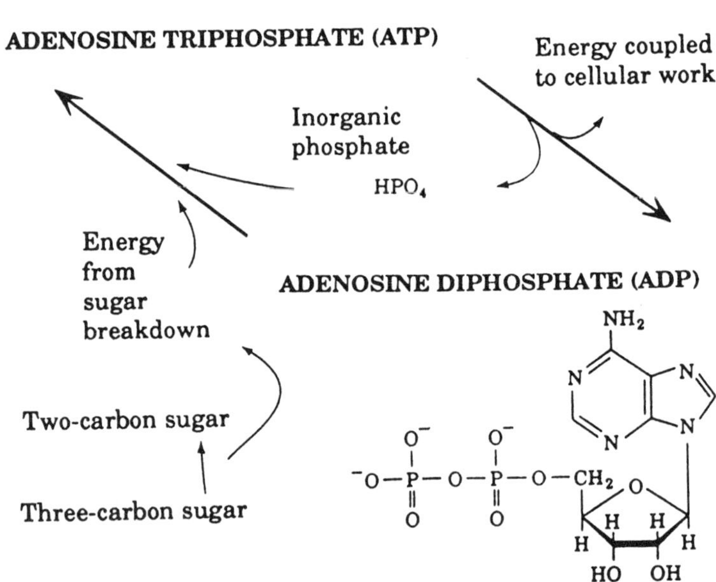

A11